WARD LOCK

FAMILY HEALTH GUIDE

DEPRESSION

DR STEPHEN MERSON

IN ASSOCIATION WITH THE
DEFEAT DEPRESSION CAMPAIGN

WARD LOCK

A WARD LOCK BOOK

First published in the UK 1995
by Ward Lock
Wellington House
125 Strand
LONDON
WC2R 0BB

A Cassell Imprint

Distributed in the United States
by Sterling Publishing Co., Inc.
387 Park Avenue South, New York, NY 10016–8810

Distributed in Australia
by Capricorn Link (Australia) Pty Ltd
2/13 Carrington Road, Castle Hill NSW 2154

A British Library Cataloguing in Publication Data block for this book may be obtained
from the British Library

ISBN 0 7063 7395 2
Designed by Lindsey Johns and typeset by The Design Revolution, Brighton
Printed and bound in Spain

Acknowledgements
Thanks are due to Life File for supplying photographs reproduced on the following pages:
2, 10, 14 (Mike Evans); 13, 28, 40 (Emma Lee); 15 (Sally Anne Fison); 23, 63, 75 (Andrew
Ward); 26 (Nigel Shuttleworth); 29 (Nicola Sutton); 31 (Juliet Highet); 32 (Keith Curtis);
44, 47, 48 (Tim Fisher); 46 (Flora Torrance); 60 (Dave Thompson); 69 (Arthur Jumper); to
the Mansell Collection for providing the photograph on page 37; and to Parkside Health
Authority for providing the photographs on pages 50, 52, 53, 56.
Cover photograph: Pictor International Limited.

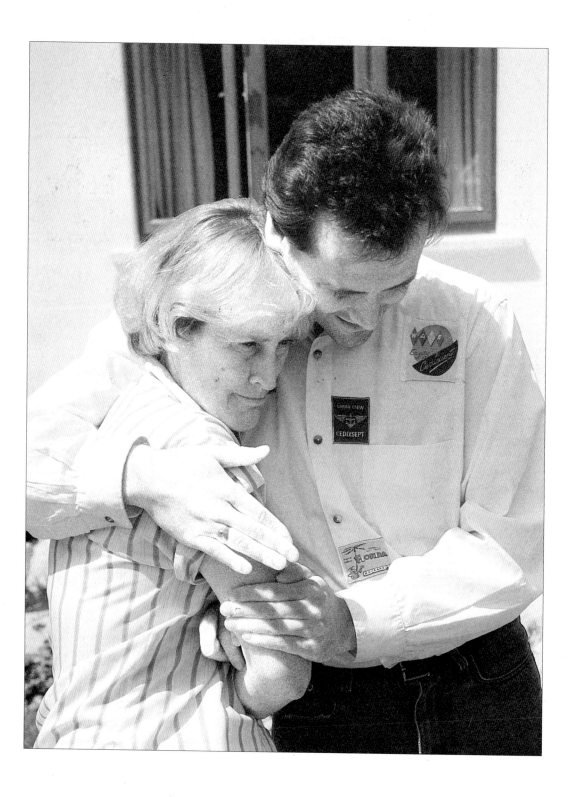

Contents

Introduction

In planning this book I tried to bear in mind the viewpoint of the general reader, and my aim was therefore to keep the text accessible and easy to use. Its purpose is first and foremost to inform and to raise awareness of depression as an illness; to clarify that it is not the same as the ordinary everyday mood changes with which we are all familiar and also that it is not always synonymous with severe or disabling mental illness such as schizophrenia or dementia; that it is not a moral failure or a source of shame; that there are very tangible and practical steps which sufferers can take to alleviate their condition and effective treatments that have been developed which will counter depression. Above all the book shows that depression is a very common problem for which there are effective forms of help at hand.

I hope that this book may prove useful both to people who are concerned that they may suffer from depression and to those who have experienced depression and possibly already received treatment. It explains how to recognize the illness, offers advice on how you can best manage in a period of depression should you be unlucky enough to find yourself in one, and how you can help someone else who is struggling because of it. The book is also for those who have experience of a friend or family member who has suffered from depression. To this end the chapters are arranged in a progressive order, headings draw attention to important areas and boxed items discuss issues which are particularly topical or contentious.

The book hopes to clarify what depression as an illness is, and what it isn't. It then aims to guide the reader, in a logical and understandable way, through the practical steps necessary to manage depression, to seek help and to ensure complete recovery.

Stephen Merson

Chapter one
Is depression an illness?

Our changing moods

Mood is actually something which affects all of us constantly, though we don't always recognize this explicitly or talk about it. We would all be prepared to admit that our own emotions and feelings vary from time to time and that this is tied up with the circumstances we meet in our day-to-day life. In fact there is two-way traffic between our life circumstances and our states of mood. Not only do things affect us adversely when they are not going smoothly, but when we are down in the dumps we are likely to perform less well in all spheres of life, whether it be managing our work or conducting our relationships. We are aware of the significance of mood and make allowances for it when planning our daily life. Who has not postponed an important decision because they felt at a low ebb, or relished the improvement in and effortlessness of their performance of tasks at work that accompany brimming self-confidence?

Taking a slightly longer perspective, we recognize that each of us has a characteristic range of emotional responses to particular circumstances: we call this temperament and regard it as a relatively unchanging component of an individual's character, through which we recognize an individual's hallmark. When asked to consider our friends' characters, we are apt unconsciously to spend some time describing their typical range of moods. Thus we often find ourselves using words such as moody, calm, volatile, anxious, tetchy and gloomy, and a hundred others. In cultures other than those of Western Europe concepts of depression and mood can appear to be less well developed and there are fewer words to describe them. European cultures and languages, however, are particularly rich in their consideration of the wide range of states of mood experienced by individuals. The depiction of moods is one of the most fundamental features of music and the visual arts, and evocative descriptions of emotion and mood are found throughout poetry and literature. As such, mood states are an important aspect of our existence, and one that we value very highly. We rightly recognize that the tonal background represented by our moods adds a vital and irreplaceable dimension to the weave of our lives.

Is depression an illness?

Depressed or just feeling low?

Unsurprisingly for such an important factor in our life, the ups and downs of mood have also attracted the interest of doctors and psychiatrists. From an early time they have been aware that certain individuals are inclined to experience exaggerated mood states which seriously affect their ability to lead a normal existence. Depression has therefore come to be recognized as a form of illness which takes its place alongside other psychiatric illnesses.

How to recognize depression

The symptoms of depression the illness, as opposed to simply feeling low, are as follows:

- Pervasive low mood and tearfulness, unresponsive to and out of keeping with current circumstances.
- Other mood changes including tension, irritability and anxiety.
- Insomnia (typically waking early).
- Reduction in appetite, weight loss and constipation.
- Lack of energy and tiredness/lack of stamina.
- Loss of libido.
- Loss of concentration/forgetfulness.
- Feelings of low self-esteem, guilt and helplessness.
- Thoughts of suicide.

It has also become clear that depression is an extremely common event. This is a self-evident truth, and it is of course possible to argue that depression should not readily or too easily be regarded as an illness: after all, it will pass, and individuals are expected to 'pull themselves together' and 'get on with it' – at least, most of the time. This does illustrate a fundamental difficulty that has always faced doctors attempting to treat people suffering from depression: the question of when depression is an illness and when it is an understandable psychological reaction to the ups and downs of life. In other words, how do doctors tell the difference between what is normal and to be expected from what is abnormal (or pathological, as doctors call it)? If they adopt a pragmatic approach, it becomes clear that depression is very common indeed: for example, if they base their judgement on whether people actually seek help by consulting their family doctor or taking time off work, or if they only regard depression as a state of mind which has been present for more than a few days and which causes measurable disability in everyday life. In fact depression is more common than a host of other complaints which we also consider to be common, such as low back pain, bronchitis and other respiratory infections, asthma and diabetes.

This has implications for the definition of the type of problem which should allow the sufferer to adopt the sick role with its attendant range of rights (for instance, to be allowed time off work) and responsibilities (for example, to

Percentage of the population suffering from depression*

	1 month	12 months	Lifetime
Male	4.2%	7.7%	12.7%
Female	7.4%	12.9%	21.3%
All	5.9%	10.3%	17.1%

*1994 figures for USA; UK figures are similar.

time it lasts are the criteria that have been most frequently used to define the type of depression that is considered an illness. However, there are forms of depression which are intermittent or chronic but less severe which are also quite disabling. Some states of depression are, helpfully from the point of view of the diagnostician, so different in quality from usual experiences of mood that there is little doubt that an illness is present. Patients describe a mood which is qualitatively unlike anything they have experienced before, often using metaphors to describe this (such as black clouds) or describing their perception of their surroundings as altered. Sometimes, though, a mood state may be considered abnormal not because it is qualitatively different but because it seems out of context, in the sense of not being plausibly the result of events or circumstances, or persisting for a lengthier period than expected.

accept the advice and treatment of doctors). This is all the more difficult because we all accept a fair amount of variation in our own moods without considering that this indicates illness but believing that it shows the success or failure of how we are living our day-to-day life.

The severity of depression and the length of

Depression as an illness

Psychiatrists and other doctors have drawn these differing strands together in order to describe a concept that can be regarded as an illness that most would recognize as such. This concept can also be regarded as the common final pathway of a range of causes of depression. This is a very traditional medical approach which involves the description of an illness as it is commonly observed to occur, and which lays the foundation for further investigation of the causes of the illness and how it may be alleviated. Depressive illness is a

good example of how many diverse individual experiences can be drawn together to describe a commonly occurring condition which is abnormal and may be expected to respond to medical and other treatments. There is admittedly an enormous variation among the ways in which different people with depression show it; nevertheless the similarities outweigh the differences and allow further knowledge about depression to be gathered. Sometimes the experience of depression can legitimately be considered an illness in its own right; at others

Is depression an illness?

Women are almost twice as likely to suffer depression as men.

it may be better viewed as but one aspect of another – perhaps more serious – illness, either psychological or in some cases with a physical cause (see Chapter three).

The experience of depression is a common one that we all suffer from time to time without seeking help for it. Depression as an illness is also extremely common. According to surveys, about 5 per cent or more of the general population show symptoms of depression at any one time. It is estimated that in any 12-month period 10 per cent of the population

will experience symptoms consistent with depressive illness, and over a lifetime this prevalence rises to 20 per cent for women and 12 per cent for men. These symptoms are of a severity that would warrant the person being regarded as significantly ill in the view of psychiatrists. Of course, not all these people consider themselves ill in the sense that they feel they need help, and relatively little is known about the reasons why some people attend doctors very readily while others soldier painfully on alone. One reason is that some of these 'illnesses' are relatively short-lasting and may be seen as understandable reactions to problematic life experiences at the time. One of the most consistent findings in studies of this sort is that women are twice as likely as men to experience (or admit to suffering from) depression.

Depression is therefore a widespread experience and a major cause of suffering. In 1990 it was estimated to have cost the economy of the United Kingdom £3 billion in lost production due to sickness absence, and a further £400 million in the cost of treatment by the health service. Suicide, which is known to be very often associated with depressive illness, remains second only to accidents as a cause of death among men in the middle years of life and therefore depression represents a considerable cause of preventable death in younger people.

Yet it also remains well known that for many years now there have been very effective treatments available which will alleviate depression in a matter of weeks and therefore prevent untold distress and anguish, will save lives lost through suicide and accidents, and which may prevent the onset of the illness again in those who suffer from it on a recurrent basis.

Why and when do people seek help for depression?

Of course, not all of the individuals that are identified by community surveys seek professional help: for many their depression will be accepted as a temporary state which is due to their life circumstances and they can gain support through their informal network of supportive family and friends. However, studies in general medical practice show that psychological problems are very common and are responsible for people visiting their family doctor in up to a third of cases. Of these depression is without doubt the most common recognizable form of psychological problem encountered by doctors in the UK or any other country and treated by them.

Depression shares many of the features of mental illness and of course is regarded as one form of mental illness; it is treated by doctors and other health professionals including those who specialize only in this area, among them psychiatrists. The spectrum of mental illness is extremely broad, and includes some illnesses which are very serious and disabling and which have a very great effect on the ability of an individual to lead anything approaching a normal life. Depression can be serious and disabling. However, much more usually it is a temporary state, although often lasting weeks or months, which can be helped and shortened in various ways, including self-help and professional help. There are many examples of individuals leading successful lives while coping with periods of depression. Winston Churchill became so familiar with the depression which returned at intervals during his life that he called it by a pet name (my black dog), yet achieved pre-eminence in his fields of politics and writing.

Chapter two

How depression affects the individual

The symptoms of depression

What are the symptoms and signs of depressive illness? Both doctors and their patients would agree that these include a pervasive and sustained change in mood, a morbid sadness or gloominess, tearfulness and worrying accompanied by a characteristic and consistent change in patterns of thought towards the themes of hopelessness, guilt and self-blame, and ultimately of self-disparagement and self-destruction. This mood may, however, assume a wide variety of forms. Let us consider some case histories.

Case 1

● An elderly woman sits day after day in her small impoverished flat. She lost her husband, to whom she had been devoted for forty years, the previous winter. She sees very few people since her daughter and her family moved to a different town because of her husband's promotion. She spends her day sitting by her window. She thinks about the past. She feels unnecessary and useless. She begins to feel that others share this view and that life is futile and unlikely to change. The world becomes an unforgiving place where she is punished for minor transgressions many years ago. She begins to believe that she is responsible for terrible crimes for which in reality she could not possibly be held culpable. She frets and worries, doesn't sleep and partly through loss of appetite and partly because she feels she deserves little food, she loses weight. She begins to feel that she may suffer from a mortal disease, a cancer or AIDS, which she begins to regard as the punishment deserved for her wickedness.

How depression affects the individual

Case 2

● Valerie was happily married until the birth of her first child. The pregnancy was uneventful from the medical point of view. The labour was long and exhausting and culminated in a caesarian section, but mother and child thereafter did well. Returning home to her husband and family, she enjoyed being the centre of attention. After her husband returned to work, Valerie at first enjoyed the new routine of the baby and the flow of visitors he attracted. After two months, however, she began to miss the interest of her job and the stimulus of her colleagues. She found baby talk uninteresting and was convinced that her husband felt the same when he came home from work. They both missed their social life and found that at home in the evening they would argue. Valerie's sleep, already broken by the baby's feeding regime, deteriorated and she felt exhausted in the day. She began turning down offers of visits from her new acquaintances and found her mother's persistent involvement only irritating. One afternoon she felt so tired and demoralized that she couldn't face going on. She decided to ask her doctor for help.

Case 3

● Gerald is twenty-five years old and he works as a delivery van driver's mate. He doesn't like his job, but does enough to get by. He has a bedsit where he doesn't like to spend too much time. Mostly he's out, either in the pub or more recently with a new crowd who are into raves and a bit of ecstasy when they can find it. He left home seven years ago and doesn't have much to do with his mother, although he sometimes thinks that he should do more – perhaps send her some money which he knows she always finds tight. He doesn't know his father, and doesn't get on with his step-father. Gerald always feels as if things could be better. He never feels completely well, and when he is on his own he feels empty and purposeless. He would like a girlfriend, but somehow things never work out. His last girlfriend complained that he was too demanding and was always miserable. He feels life is passing him by and after his last girlfriend dropped him he took an overdose of aspirin and ended up being admitted to hospital.

All these people can be said to suffer from depression and all would be likely to receive a diagnosis of depression if they were to see a doctor. But what are the features that they share in common? Central to these problems is a disturbance of their usual mood which may incorporate elements usually associated with depression including sadness, misery and tearfulness. It may, however, also extend to include features more commonly associated by professionals with anxiety, or of irritability. These include worrying and overconcern, self-consciousness and phobic avoidance (avoidance of situations known to provoke fear, such as social gatherings or crowded places), sensitivity, argumentativeness and hostility. Characteristic patterns of thinking accompany these mood changes and result in the world being viewed in an excessively pessimistic or hopeless light, or in the individuals judging themselves harshly and attributing self-blame inappropriately. Such preoccupations may logically lead a person to suicidal thinking, and the danger of self-destructive acts is real.

15

How depression affects the individual

How depression may affect the body's rhythms

Another group of symptoms characteristic of depression can be considered as changes to bodily functions or rhythms. These are known as biological or somatic symptoms and are notable particularly in the more severe forms of depression. They include changes to several bodily activities which in themselves can be quite distressing and disabling. Sleep may be disrupted either by delay in falling asleep or by waking early, or by frequent repeated waking at intervals through the night. Whatever the pattern, the refreshing quality of sleep is lost. Patients often describe a physical loss of energy or stamina which it is possible to distinguish from the loss of motivation, enthusiasm and enjoyment which may, of course, be evident. They may nevertheless persist doggedly with greater efforts yet still fail to manage adequately. This lethargy may be apparent to others as listlessness and slowness in initiating activity, and in a reduction in the number of changes in bodily posture and facial expression of which we all have a recognizable repertoire. The individual finds it increasingly difficult to concentrate and to attend to mental tasks, and this may appear as forgetfulness or frequent mistakes. Appetite for food may be reduced, food becomes tasteless and is ignored and, over a period of time, weight loss occurs; the patient may be aware of constipation and nausea. Interest in sexual activity is often diminished, both because of inability to give affection and because of physical disinclination; some men may experience impotence and women's periods may become irregular or cease.

The effect of depression on our thinking

Characteristic patterns of thinking (or cognition) accompany the mood changes of depression, and this in itself can lead to changes in behaviour that may be noticeable to friends and family. People who are depressed tend to view the world in an excessively pessimistic or hopeless light; there is no expectation that matters will improve and often this dismal state of affairs is perceived by the sufferers as being their own responsibility. More generally the individuals judge themselves harshly and underestimate their own positive attributes in favour of this self-disparaging and critical view. Such thoughts may range from a scarcely noticeable pessimistic tainting of normal statements and opinions to unpleasant and unwelcome preoccupations which make life a misery. These might include ideas of sinfulness and wickedness, ideas which are quite out of proportion and which may reach delusional intensity (i.e. be perceived by others to be obviously false). Such preoccupations may logically lead individuals to thoughts of delivering themselves from such a shameful or tormenting situation by ending their life, and suicidal behaviour and the danger of self-destructive acts are real.

Effects on daily routine

How is such an illness likely to affect ordinary individuals and their daily routine? Depression is not like arthritis or asthma in affecting a single, well-defined, bodily system. Depression has effects on the person as a whole, and when thinking of the disabilities associated with depression it is useful to consider the roles which most of us fulfil during each day of our life. Thus in terms of work depressed individuals are liable to be slow and less productive, to be indecisive and uncertain, and to make more mistakes. At home they will lack interest in their family and will be unable to enjoy their company and shared activities, and to participate in family life. They will be unable to demonstrate affection for loved ones and uninterested in love-making. They will tend to avoid friends and social gatherings, and be unable to derive satisfaction from hobbies and leisure interests.

The more severe the illness, the greater the disability. Individuals suffering from a mild form of illness would be distressed by their symptoms but able to continue activities in all areas of life albeit with greater efforts. With increasing symptoms, performance of social, work and domestic activities becomes possible only with significantly greater effort until, in severe illnesses, activity beyond the short-term keeping of body and soul together becomes quite impossible. In this situation the very evident and immediate risk of self-neglect or suicide may necessitate the level of supervision and care that can be provided only in hospital.

Over the years, particularly the last thirty, psychiatrists have reached agreement with respect to the type of symptoms which lead to the diagnosis of depressive illness. The great advantage of this is that all psychiatrists now mean the same thing by the use of the term as well as allowing researchers to describe the conditions they are examining more consistently. Most psychiatrists would accept the criteria of the World Health Organisation (1991) which require the patient to experience, over a period of at least two weeks, sustained alteration of mood, loss of interest and enjoyment, and a tendency to feel tired all the time, together with two or more of the seven following features: reduced concentration, reduced self-esteem, ideas of unworthiness or guilt, pessimism, ideas or acts of self-harm or suicide, reduced sleep and diminished appetite. This has the advantage of fairly accurately portraying the type of depression which most psychiatrists would recognize as being an illness, likely to limit the activity of the individual, and liable also to be responsive to treatment. At the same time it allows differentiation from other illnesses where mood disturbances are a feature but which are separate from depression and may call for different treatments (see Chapter three).

Chapter three
The different types of depression

Depression, as defined in Chapter two, can adopt quite a wide variety of disguises and is generally recognized as including a range of different disorders. Studies of the outcome, causes and treatment of depression have tended to play down the differences and instead consider depression as a single illness. As such the syndrome of depressive illness described in Chapter one represents a basic building block of psychiatric thinking. It is a group of symptoms which appear to occur naturally in association and which, if left untreated, may last for a period of several months before disappearing spontaneously. This we know from so-called naturalistic studies carried out in the period before effective treatment was the norm, when it was possible to observe patients over long periods of time (this sort of study would be considered unethical nowadays). It has also come to be regarded as a final common pathway of a range of environmental and constitutional circumstances which are all known to be involved in the causation of depression.

Depression and other physical and mental illnesses

Depression can occur in association with and perhaps as a consequence of certain physical/medical conditions (epilepsy, stroke, Parkinson's disease, hormonal imbalance, and the effects of psycho-active and therapeutic drugs, for example, are all well known to be able to produce an illness indistinguishable from depression). It can also occur in the context of other psychiatric conditions which are generally reckoned to be more serious than depression, such as schizophrenia and dementia. Psychiatrists would consider depression in these circumstances to be secondary to the more 'important' condition, and treatment would therefore be directed at the latter and would follow the guidelines for this associated condition with the expectation that the depression would lift as other symptoms simultaneously responded.

The core of purely depressive illnesses that cannot be attributable to any other illness is often known by doctors in shorthand as major depression, clinical depression or depressive illness. It still includes a very wide range of conditions, particularly with regard to their severity and impact on the sufferer's life. The

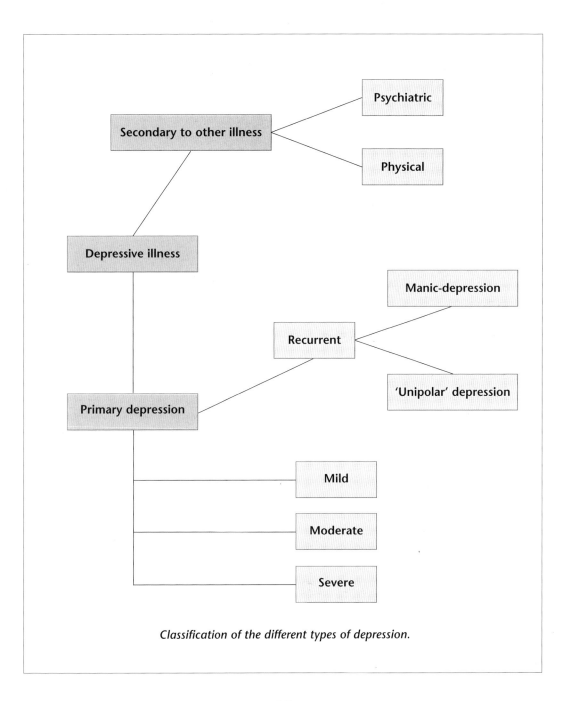

Classification of the different types of depression.

The different types of depression

range extends from severe illnesses, where activity is greatly curtailed and thinking and perception are as distorted as in forms of insanity such as schizophrenia, to milder forms which seem closer in character to the time-limited reactions to untoward events in our lives during which we expect to experience fluctuations from our normal patterns of mood and motivation. The terms 'stress reaction' and 'adjustment disorders' are used by doctors to describe succinctly these less pathological (abnormal) reactions.

How, then, have psychiatrists attempted to understand these illnesses and their causation? Research into depression has arisen from several different angles and these are described more fully in Chapter nine. The scientific disciplines involved range across an enormous landscape of the human sciences from the biological and medical sciences to those of psychology and sociology, which accounts for the possibility of several theories approaching a problem like depression from apparently different perspectives. This can be confusing, but need not be so. It is often helpful to view a knotty problem from several angles before a solution presents itself, whether the problem is,

say, a car that will not start (lack of petrol; flat battery; broken starter motor, etc.) or a depressed person. Many factors may be involved in the onset of depression in any individual, ranging from bodily constitution to style of coping with difficulties to the amount of family support. If we therefore remember that there are different sides to every coin, a genetic view is no longer inconsistent with a social theory in order to explain what has happened. Certainly in practice, when treating patients with depression, it is possible to recognize several plausible causative factors and to consider logically more than one type of treatment which can be expected to work cumulatively for the benefit of the patient. Depressive illness can best be seen as a final common pathway of a potentially rather large number of influences and factors acting upon the constitution of individuals in their particular social context.

As in the case of any common condition, particular sub-groups have been recognized over the years. Although knowledge of what these distinctions mean may be limited at present, such divisions may lead to improved understanding of cause, course and treatment.

Common forms of depression

Melancholia and psychotic depression

These more severe forms of depression are frequently seen by psychiatrists, although they are, in the wider context of general medical practice, rather rare. These illnesses share many

of the features of psychiatric disorders traditionally considered as more serious than most depressions. Patients may develop beliefs about themselves and the world about them which are false, at times bizarrely and obviously so. Typically sufferers of severe

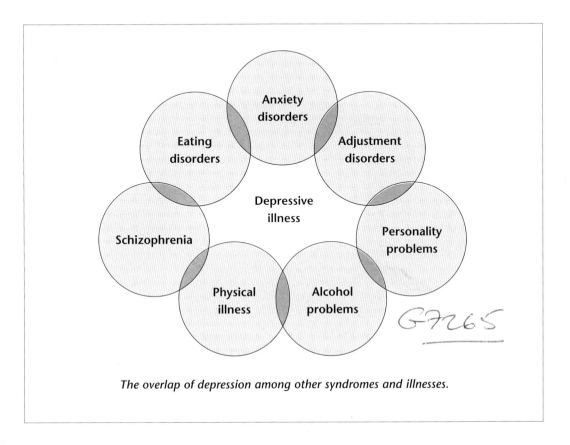

The overlap of depression among other syndromes and illnesses.

depression may become convinced that they are guilty of shameful deeds or crimes which they could not possibly be responsible for, such as a war or a natural catastrophe. They may believe that they are suffering from a terminal illness, and may interpret other symptoms of depression, such as weight loss or constipation, as proof of this. They may feel that others view them as worthless wretches and may feel they deserve their torment as a just punishment. Consistent with these beliefs, sufferers may hallucinate voices which pour scorn on, insult or threaten them, or urge them to commit suicide, or they may see terrifying hallucinated apparitions of the devil.

Naturally such people may quite easily not recognize that they are ill, and because they are at risk of serious self-neglect through failing to eat or drink, or failing to care for their hygiene, or in some cases be greatly at risk of a suicidal act, they may require hospital admission. Sometimes for their own protection this is on a compulsory basis. In these cases depression is a seriously debilitating and potentially life-threatening illness and recovery from it is often delayed and incomplete.

The different types of depression

Manic-depressive illness

A group of sufferers from recurrent depression is also known to at other times suffer from a condition known as mania. Mania is in many ways the mirror image of depression. It is characterized by periods during which the patients are elated in mood, expansive and confident in their ideas, and full of energy and enthusiasm. This group of patients is described as suffering from manic-depressive illness or bipolar disorder and they represent a relatively small proportion of sufferers from depressive illnesses, but are important. This is because the age of onset of these disorders is early, often in the middle twenties as opposed to the average age of onset for all depression which is in the middle thirties, and therefore the potential for suffering and adverse effects on the sufferers' life are magnified. Also these conditions are severe and tend to be recurrent.

Manic-depressive illnesses tend to run more in families than most depressions and also to be more severe as well as recurrent. Sometimes they can be dangerous, disruptive of home and business life, and often lead to hospital admission. Sufferers are often treated with drugs, which are generally effective in controlling the symptoms of the disorder, and which also tend to be recommended as longer-term protection against recurrence.

Depression and anxiety

Anxiety is a common symptom of depressive illness as well as of other disorders. It can be shown by both psychological and bodily symptoms. The former include fearfulness, panic attacks, worrying and avoidance of situations which experience shows induce fear (these are phobias or irrational avoidance and fear of harmless situations). Physical effects of anxiety include breathing difficulties, palpitation, sweating, trembling and feelings of bodily tension. It is not unusual for these symptoms to occur in depressed people and indeed at times to dominate the pattern of symptoms. However, careful enquiry often allows the typical features of depression, such as insomnia, which thereby allows the correct diagnosis to be made.

Depression and physical symptoms

Depression has many features which are intensely physical in nature. Many of these symptoms and signs are very similar to symptoms seen in diseases which are known to have an identifiable physical cause. These symptoms include aches and pains, weight loss, constipation, tiredness, loss of appetite and others. It can therefore be difficult for both patients and doctors to be certain whether a physical symptom is representative of depression, or alternatively suggests an entirely different disorder that may need further tests and investigations which may show the existence of an illness requiring quite a different treatment.

In addition, because it is sometimes considered unacceptable to be psychologically disturbed, physical symptoms are occasionally used as substitutes for psychological symptoms, particularly the more minor variations in mood. Many cultures express mood changes in concrete bodily terms, including descriptions of

Anxiety is a common symptom of depressive illness as well as of other disorders.

The different types of depression

pains, for example. Many patients feel that doctors are trained to respond to bodily complaints and hence present these unconsciously to their doctors. It is well known that common physical complaints can have a psychological contribution. Headaches, for instance, can be made worse by the increase in muscular tension of the neck and scalp muscles which are a physical accompaniment of a state of anxiety. In the more severe forms of depression not only are very physical symptoms such as slowness and constipation more to the fore, but worries about their physical state can increase in people until they imagine they are ill when they are not, sometimes to the point of serious delusion. As depression intensifies, a patient may go through the stages of suffering a tension headache, to worrying that this same symptom might represent a brain tumour, to being convinced that God has seen fit to punish past wickedness by destroying their brain.

Depression with reversed biological symptoms

As described above, the commonest forms of depression are characterized by a general lowering of the level of activity whether this is shown by a fall in appetite, a loss of sleep, or a reduction in activities. Paradoxically a few depressed patients experience a reversal of this usual pattern and therefore find themselves sleeping more, though not generally feeling refreshed and energetic as a result, and eating more and consequently tending to gain weight. These patients' illnesses may be missed by doctors and the true significance of their

symptoms not recognized, so that treatment may be delayed or withheld.

Recurrent brief depression

It has recently become recognized that quite large numbers of the population experience periods of depression which, while not lasting for long enough to be generally regarded as a depressive illness by the usual criteria (see Chapter one), do bring in their wake significant problems. These individuals suffer from mood changes lasting a few days only. At its most extreme such a pattern of mood disturbance can lead to serious albeit impulsive attempts at self-harm, which of course may be fatal, but it will also cause difficulties in, for example, employment and relationships. This type of depression is currently subject to a considerable amount of research interest aimed at determining its relationship to other forms of depression (for instance, does it lead to longer periods of depression later in life?) and its usual course and response to treatment.

Adjustment disorders

We are all familiar with the feeling of depression, which may also be accompanied by other experiences such as lack of interest in food, lethargy, apathy and inertia, which follows a major disappointment such as failing to pass an examination or to secure a promotion. Our experience tells us that certain life events seem intuitively to be more threatening and unsettling than others. Very often such events contain an element of a loss, whether this be a tangible loss such as the death of a loved one or the break-up of a relationship, or a more symbolic loss such as the surrender of an aspiration or a valued ambition. We expect to be affected by such happenings, and the pattern of mood changes is very similar to those seen in depression, and indeed at times may be prolonged and be considered as such. Usually, however, symptoms would be expected to improve with simple measures such as expressing feelings about the distressing event. Psychiatrists call this reaction a stress reaction to distinguish it from depressive illness which may require a different treatment approach. Interestingly this concept overlaps considerably with the previously described notion of recurrent brief depression, and there is interest in the relationship between the two concepts.

Chronic depression and dysthymia

Recent study of the occurrence of depression and dysthymia (a less severe form of the illness) in the general population has identified sub-groups of people who experience symptoms of depression which do not correspond to the widely accepted stereotype of the depressive illness, but which nevertheless appear significant in terms of the distress and disability that they cause to the sufferers. These people show slightly different patterns of symptoms. Often they have long-standing though relatively mild symptoms which nevertheless interfere with their ability to lead life as they wish. They persistently lack enthusiasm, motivation and the ability to enjoy.

Another group experiences intense depressive symptoms but which last only a short time, often just a matter of a few days. During this period they show enough symptoms that, if a doctor is consulted, depression is generally diagnosed. Indeed they are at risk of self-harm during this time and often come to medical attention because of an unsuccessful suicide attempt. However, the depression lifts very rapidly without treatment and in retrospect the brief, though dramatic, disturbance of mood does not appear to be associated with adverse life events and difficulties that might otherwise be expected. As yet it is not clear how this group responds to conventional treatments for depression, but it appears to be a large and important group which has hitherto not received much attention.

Depression and schizophrenia

Schizophrenia has been viewed as a distinct entity from depressive illness since at least the late nineteenth century, and there is much evidence supportive of this view. Yet it is also true that patients who have been diagnosed as suffering from schizophrenia may at times, during the course of their illness, suffer from significant and discomforting depressive symptoms. This is most often the case in patients suffering from so-called negative schizophrenia. The negative symptoms that give this syndrome its name describe a series of deficits and are in many ways similar to the symptoms of depression. Thus these patients lack motivation, are lethargic, find it difficult to concentrate and experience a restricted range of emotional responses, which is very evident to others around them. The treatment of their

The different types of depression

As autumn comes and the days grow shorter, people living in the northern hemisphere are more likely to suffer from seasonal affective disorder.

symptoms, however, requires quite a different approach from the treatment used for the symptoms of 'ordinary' depressive illness.

Another group of sufferers from schizophrenia experience mood disturbances including depression in the aftermath of their illness; this is often associated with a realization of the implications of their illness for their long-term well-being.

Depression and alcohol abuse

Pharmacologically speaking, alcohol is in the short term a stimulant drug. It is valued in our society because it makes us more confident socially and allows us to appear more witty and attractive than normal. However, in the longer term it acts as a depressant. Several hours after drinking alcohol we feel tired, drowsy and sluggish. It may also disrupt our sleep pattern, bringing further effects in its wake, including the hangover that is so well known. If alcohol is persistently abused, it can lead to a state of depression that can be quite long-lasting and also quite debilitating. Usually if the damage to an individual's work, marriage and finances are not great, this damage can be repaired and mood will return to normal once the person abstains. It is of course the case that those who have problems with alcohol are generally using the drug to correct some rather chronic state of unhappiness, although in the long run this is certainly a self-defeating strategy.

Seasonal affective disorder

It has long been observed that the incidence of depression varies with the seasons. For example, depression and suicide seem to be more frequent in the population during the spring months in men but more common in the autumn and winter in women. In the 1980s a small group of patients considered to be suffering from manic-depressive illnesses (that is, a tendency to suffer episodes of both depression and mania – its opposite – at different times) were noted to follow a cyclical pattern with depressions in the winter and mania in the summer. It was also noted that latitude had an effect on these illnesses in that moving north made depression worse and moving south had a beneficial effect (at least, for those living in the northern hemisphere). This group of patients seems to derive benefit from light therapy which involves a daily exposure for two hours to light of an intensity of a bright summer day, although this finding has never been rigorously tested. Nevertheless the term seasonal affective disorder (SAD) has been coined to describe this small group of sufferers.

Depression and HIV

With the epidemic of HIV and AIDS in recent years attention has focused on the effects on mood and depression. In common with other life-threatening illnesses, positive HIV status and AIDS itself can be involved as factors in provoking depression in their own right. HIV infection also carries with it other potent adverse connotations including a degree of social stigma, the risk of losing other loved ones including partners, and financial problems. It has also become apparent that the HIV virus itself can produce mood changes directly. The virus is known to invade the

The different types of depression

central nervous system preferentially and may lead to changes in the brain similar to those found in Alzheimer's disease and other forms of dementia. Even before this stage of the illness, depression may be a feature. There are therefore several ways in which HIV can cause an individual to become depressed and this is likely to remain an important area of research for some time to come.

Depression in women

It has long been noticed that women are over-represented in the group of sufferers from depression. In all the studies to date they consistently appear to outnumber their depressed male counterparts by a ratio of two to one. By contrast the numbers of men and women seeking treatment for depression is roughly equivalent. Why is this? It may be that women are more readily detected as depressed than men, who tend to soldier on. Women generally have more extensive networks of social supports and confidants, which has been shown to be an effective source of help for those with depression: men, who are relatively lacking in this resource, may more readily turn

Women generally enjoy a more extensive network of social supports and confidants than men.

to professionals for help. Finally it may be true that women are more likely to suffer from depression, either because of inherent constitutional reasons (though there is no evidence to support this view and it would be currently unfashionable) or because of their relative social disadvantage. In addition there are experiences which by their very nature are restricted to women.

Pregnancy seems to be a period of relative mental well-being for women, but it appears to be compensated for by an increased vulnerability to depression following the birth of a child. Such post-natal depression, as it is called, needs to be differentiated from the short-lived feelings of emotional turmoil which occur in up to one-third of new mothers in the week after delivery (the 'baby blues'). Post-natal depression in contrast typically has an onset somewhat later, in the first three months, and is in its features not obviously different from other forms of depression. It would also be expected to respond to similar treatments, although some care is required in prescribing drug treatments if the mother is breast-feeding, since most drugs taken by the mother enter her milk. For most anti-depressant drugs this is not harmful, but lithium treatment should not be given unless the mother is prepared to relinquish breast-feeding.

Post-natal depression also needs to be distinguished from the more serious puerperal psychosis, which is less common. This is a potentially severe form of illness which shares some characteristics with depression but also involves experiences such as delusions and perceptual abnormalities, such as

Women can be particularly vulnerable to depression following the birth of a child.

hallucinations, which are potentially serious in terms of the effects on the predictability of the mother's behaviour.

Post-natal depression is associated more frequently than would normally be expected with ante-natal problems (such as eclampsia), complicated labours and caesarean deliveries. It is more common in women with a previous episode of post-natal depression, in women who are uncertain or unhappy about having a child, and in those who lack support in the form of a confiding relationship, including single mothers. Why women are prone to depression at this time is not clear, although from our knowledge of the causes of depression in general it is easy to see several potential causes operating in this case. The time around childbirth is clearly one of immense biological upheaval, including rapid and sustained

The different types of depression

alteration in the endocrine environment (sudden increases in prolactin and decreases in oestrogens and progestagens – hormones associated with reproduction), culminating in a period of physical ordeal not unlike a major illness, with the threat of illness and even death for mother and child. The arrival of a child, particularly the first, is not only a major change in a woman's lifestyle, in terms of altered roles and social networks, but also may bring to the surface dormant conflicts related to her own parenting so many years ago and is therefore a potent symbolic event.

Women experience significant depressive symptoms at particular times of their menstrual cycle too. Pre-menstrual syndrome (PMS) or pre-menstrual tension (PMT) typically occurs during the time – as much as two weeks before – leading up to a menstrual period, at which point symptoms disappear. Symptoms are often physical, such as feelings of bloatedness, tiredness, headache and breast tenderness, but psychological symptoms are very common and indeed characteristic. Irritability, tearfulness, anxiety and depression following such a clear-cut pattern should not be treated with anti-depressant drugs. Nevertheless these symptoms can constitute a significant problem and treatment with oestrogen administered through skin patches is likely to provide relief.

Depression in children and adolescents

Depression as an illness in children appears to be relatively rare. Depressed mood by contrast is associated with a wide variety of childhood problems, ranging from bereavement and physical illness to stressful life events including school bullying and pressure of school work. Depressive illness has an equal sex distribution and is usually treated by methods involving the family rather than by drug treatments, except in the more severe cases. Childhood problems such as bed-wetting or school truanting were previously often regarded as masked forms of depression, but are now considered to be separate from depressive illness.

Although the adolescent years are generally looked upon as a time of emotional upheaval ('adolescent turmoil') during which depression frequently occurs, in fact the vast majority of teenagers are happy and depression as an illness is rather rare in this age group. This remains so despite the major changes experienced during adolescence in terms of physical and sexual maturity, young people finding their identity as individuals within the family and expectations that adult rules will be adopted. What is of current concern is the rising rate of suicidal behaviour, particularly among boys in this group and among the slightly older group of young adults, which contrasts with the generally declining rates in all other age groups. Also of concern is the realization that depression beginning at such an early stage is likely to be severe and recurrent and it is therefore important that it is detected and treated effectively. Symptoms are in quality not different from those of adult depression, although irritability and social withdrawal may be prominent, and discordant family relationships also noticeable.

Despite the physical and emotional upheavals of adolescence, depression as an illness is not common among teenagers.

The different types of depression

Many elderly people enjoy living life to the full, but the results of studies show that the likelihood of depression increases with age.

Depression in the elderly

Rates of new cases of depression increase with the age of the population being studied. There are several plausible reasons why this may be so. Physical illness is more common in older people and some diseases such as strokes frequently cause depression. Old age is also a time of change and particularly of loss – of status and position in society, wealth, opportunity, friends and spouses. Illnesses are also likely to be more severe, and to respond to treatment less favourably. They are more often treated with physical methods such as drugs; and also, particularly where depression is extremely severe, is causing delusions or is life-threatening, electro-convulsive therapy (ECT) is liable to provide a safe and rapidly effective treatment.

Unusual forms of depression sometimes occur in this age group. Excessive worrying about non-existent or very minor health problems, or attention-seeking behaviour, or intense anxiety may often hide other symptoms of depression. Pseudo-dementia is the name given by doctors to a type of depression which appears superficially as a problem with memory and which is relatively common in older people and may be confused with the presence of dementia. (Dementia is the term applied to illnesses where memory and other higher mental functions are affected and includes illnesses such as Alzheimer's disease.) In pseudo-dementia, patients' memory appears to be affected, but closer examination will reveal that they are inattentive to their surroundings and hence unable to retain new information in the form of new memories. Their slowness and apathy is, of course, similar to the effects of dementia. The significance is that depression in this age group, unlike dementia, can generally be successfully treated if recognized.

Chapter four

How depression was viewed in the past

The origin of depression as an illness is far from easy to trace accurately. Ideas concerning mental derangements went through many changes during early times and often were not clearly differentiated from physical diseases. Mind and body were considered to be more intimately connected then than we generally allow nowadays.

The influence of humours and demons

From the time of the fifth-century-BC Greek doctor Hippocrates, arguably the founder of modern medical thought, until the late Middle Ages, ideas concerning the origin of disease were based upon the theory of the humours, or bodily fluids. According to this the character of an individual was the result of the proportions in which he or she was endowed with the four bodily humours: blood, yellow bile, black bile and phlegm. Each humour was thought to be associated with one of the elements (earth, air, fire and water) and also with its corresponding temperament or character. For example, individuals in which the humour blood dominated were associated with the choleric temperament and those with an excess of water with the melancholic. Extremes of temperament and their associated cluster of illnesses were envisaged as the result of imbalances in the proportions of the humours. In fact many of the words we use today to describe mood states implicitly hark back to these notions. For instance, we talk about bilious attacks as being outpourings of envy and hatred, and phlegmatic individuals who are unflappable and difficult to excite.

Such ideas were not seriously challenged and remained in vogue until the late Middle Ages. In the seventeenth century, in keeping with the expansion of the role of the church into moral and secular life, there emerged views of mental illness based heavily upon demonic activity and possession and witchcraft. Insanity in all its forms was seen as the result of possession of an individual by external and diabolical forces. Treatments for the patient such as exorcism and purging were administered by the clergy in addition to their more usual pastoral activities. With the Reformation this notion was neatly adjusted by

the hierarchy of church and state threatened by the rise of Protestantism by introducing the idea of religious enthusiasm, a perversity or excess of religious zeal leading to mental illness.

An individual problem

In the following centuries the rise of secularism challenged the role of the church in the care and control of the mentally ill. The source of mental illness generally was believed now to lie within the individual rather than being imposed by outside forces. The attentions of the earlier professionals concerned with mental illness began to concentrate upon the thoughts, motives and experiences of individuals as opposed to merely their observable behaviour, laying the groundwork for modern psychiatry. Ideas, for example, of visitation by the devil or the holy spirit, which in the seventeenth century would have been regarded, if not as quite an everyday occurrence, at least as not indicating serious derangement, were now seen as delusions, the quintessence of madness. This led directly to the approach of the nineteenth century – the classification of psychiatric disorders alongside other illnesses, by which twentieth-century psychiatrists remain heavily influenced.

The nineteenth century saw great advances in science; in the medical field huge strides were made in microbiology and pathology and subsequently the cause of many common and serious physical ailments was discovered. This prompted not only a surge in theorizing as to the causes of mental illness, but also the

appearance of several proposed treatments for mental illnesses, many of which seem ludicrous by today's standards. Treatments in the nineteenth century included purging, bleeding and cooling and are in direct line to the more technologically advanced treatments such as insulin coma therapy for schizophrenia in the middle of this century. (The last involved giving patients insulin to lower blood sugar levels and induce a comatose state over several hours.)

It is true that some psychological disturbances were found to be associated with somatic or cerebral pathology, the best-known example being general paralysis of the insane which was discovered to be the result of tertiary (advanced) syphilis. Many other theories, however, turned out not to be so fruitful. Depression, in common with many other psychiatric disorders, came to be regarded as a neuro-degenerative condition (that is, one in which the nervous system is irreversibly damaged), an idea incidentally bound up with the eugenic concept of moral degeneration – the notion that many diseases were largely genetically determined and their appearance in a family heralded its 'moral' decline. This was based upon the concept of cyclical degeneration and regeneration of vigour over succeeding generations. Depression would have

How depression was viewed in the past

been regarded as an early stage of an inevitable process of intellectual and moral decline ending in mental handicap or mental incompetence in later generations.

Building on many of these advances and concepts, this century has seen the establishment of the study and treatment of mental illness as the rightful domain of medicine. It was during this period that careful and painstaking description of the features of mental illness has led to knowledge of the course and outcome of the common and serious disorders, and to the experimental evaluation of proposed treatments. Linked to advances in the twentieth century in neuro-biological sciences, effective treatments for many mental illnesses, not least depression, have been discovered, tried and tested.

From Freud to the present day

Sigmund Freud (1856–1939) and his followers, who were interested in the psychological causes of mental illness and whose philosophical origins can be traced back to the eighteenth century, in contrast developed theories concerning psychological causation on an individual level. This represented part of a wider-ranging reaction among intellectuals against the prevailing tide of determinism, which considered that the fate of individuals was pre-determined by their genes and constitution. The new thinking allowed the influence for better or worse by their experiences in life, particularly those occurring earlier on. Although accepting that, literally speaking, it was impossible to turn back the clock, shedding light on some of these formative experiences would free individuals and give them the ability to alter the path their life would take. This was based upon the notion that part of the mind holds drives and beliefs which are kept from the conscious knowledge of individuals but which nevertheless influence their behaviour.

Psychological treatments which enabled these unconscious aspects of the mind to be delved into with the help of a therapist, and mentally reliving traumatic childhood events, were proposed as able to adjust faulty patterns of behaviour in adult life.

In much the same way the circumstances in which individuals lived their life were seen to affect their psychological well-being, and it became acceptable to consider unemployment, social adversity, housing problems, relationships and social support to be important in the same way. Taken in conjunction with advances in studies of the collective role of societal factors, these two strands have come together in modern treatments for depression. It is now usual for depression to be regarded as a group of closely related disorders with a range of overlapping potential causes. The identification of past personal adversity as well as current social problems is nowadays seen as leading to potentially important interventions in the treatment of depression.

Sigmund Freud, the founder of psychoanalysis, had immense influence upon modern thought.

Chapter five

Depression in others – how you can help

To what extent do sufferers notice their depression? Usually the effects are only too obvious as individuals become aware of the changed way they are feeling, or of symptoms such as sleep or appetite disturbance. Other more subtle manifestations can often go unrecognized rather than unnoticed. These include irritability, anxiety and worrying, particularly if they come on the individual in an insidious or gradual fashion, or if their effects are disguised by social withdrawal or reliance upon alcohol (which, of course, may lead to different problems of its own). In these circumstances depression comes to light only because friends or family members notice a change in the behaviour of the individual and are able to bring it to their attention. This behaviour can vary from lack of enjoyment of usual pastimes to failure to carry out responsibilities or a more general change in demeanour. Occasionally our workmates or colleagues will notice a change in our performance at work and are in a good position to bring this sympathetically to our attention. Correspondingly for people who live and work alone depression is likely to go unrecognized

and to become more protracted.

What is likely to happen once it has been accepted that someone is not at their best and may be depressed? We all behave differently in various circumstances and our responses to this situation also tend to vary widely – after all, each of us is unique. Because of this the experience of depression will bring out different responses in different individuals. At one extreme are people who may worry excessively, imagine they are seriously ill and plague their doctor for help, advice and reassurance. At the other are those who steadfastly resist accepting themselves as ill and soldier painfully on despite the growing evidence that they are failing badly. There is also an understandable tendency to deny or downplay the existence of a problem such as depression: this is because in our society mental illness is still often regarded as a moral weakness. In addition the temptation to try to see depression as a consequence of the action of outside circumstances rather than any frailty in ourselves is appealing as it tends to suggest that the problem is less serious and threatening. It does, however, encourage sufferers to battle on needlessly alone and avoid seeking help when this might actually be useful and lead to a solution to the problem. The balance in all these cases lies between encouraging an individual to remain positive at the same time as facilitating their access to an appropriate form of extra help while they are depressed.

Adjusting

Some individuals will therefore undoubtedly need encouragement in order to regard themselves as ill and to seek the help that they need. But what steps should we take? When depressed, we need temporarily to adjust our lifestyle so that important activities are not adversely affected by our depression and we are not overwhelmed with responsibilities, complex tasks and difficult decisions which we are unlikely to perform to the best of our ability. In other cases where individuals may remain unaware of the changes in their behaviour and mood, their failing performance and their withdrawal from normal activities, family, friends, workmates and employers are well placed to notice such changes and to enquire sympathetically of the sufferer so that temporary changes can be made.

Masked depression

Occasionally depression remains masked. An individual is able to keep up a brave face, and to compensate for his or her lethargy and distractedness by increasingly greater conscious efforts. In these instances depression may reveal itself in unusual ways. Individuals may develop problem drinking as a result of attempting to drown their sorrows (alcohol is in the short-term a mood stimulant, but ultimately a depressant drug). Alternatively depression may show itself as unconventional, uninhibited or histrionic behaviour, or as forms of risk-taking. The latter may include gambling, or behaviour of a sexual or minor criminal nature which is inconsistent with the individual's reputation and social standing. Occasionally more openly self-destructive behaviour, which may be seen as a way of drawing attention to the sufferer's plight, is the feature which attracts attention.

Helping friends and family who are depressed

Perhaps for some of the reasons mentioned above it may be difficult for someone suffering from depression to acknowledge a problem and seek help. Others who may come into contact with this type of situation need to know what the best approach to such an individual is.

Depression in others – how you can help

Pretending that there is not a problem is not an effective response, since the problem is likely to remain, at least in the short term. Equally it is important to avoid reacting in a negative fashion to a depressed individual, which will only make the problem worse. It is very easy to become impatient with a slow and hesitant person, or to respond with further arguments to their complaining intolerance. The gloominess of depression can be mistaken for self-pity and cause others to urge the sufferer to pull themselves together (this is doomed to failure), or to remark that they are not pulling their weight which serves only to make them feel even more guilty than they may do already.

If you suspect that a friend is depressed and want to help, the first step must be to encourage them to describe their situation.

The first step must be to encourage the person to describe their situation. The most effective way of doing so is through patient and sympathetic listening which allows painful sentiments to be voiced. Make it clear that you are available and willing to help. This can be a great support in itself and may also allow the sufferer to accept the problem and share this burden, even to a small extent, and begin to believe that something can be done to alleviate their position.

This sounds straightforward, but is in fact far from easy. It helps to become knowledgeable about depression generally and about how it affects your particular friend or relative. Be aware that it may be difficult for them to speak to someone emotionally close, perhaps for fear of being a further burden and also because there may be worry lest relatives feel guilty that they have somehow let down their depressed relative. Many depressed people find it difficult to respond warmly to the well-intentioned enquiries of a friend, and the consciousness of this very inability can be a source of further suffering.

Don't rush in with instant solutions

It is important to avoid the temptation of bland and premature reassurance: this merely encourages the sufferer to believe that you are not taking their problem seriously. It is equally important to avoid accepting too readily plausible reasons for the depression. This is because it is sometimes simply not possible to attribute a single cause or even a group of factors as the cause, and this approach also

> ## How to help a depressed person
>
> - Be tactful, but not to the point of pretending that the problem does not exist.
> - Seek an opportunity to communicate that you are aware of the person's difficulty and available to help or listen.
> - Invite the person to express how he or she is feeling, but do not insist on it.
> - Do not demand too much: be encouraging but patient, allowing the person to choose his or her pace.
> - Try to avoid premature or bland reassurance, which risks communicating that you fail to understand or do not care.
> - Make it clear that you are trying to understand and ask what you can do.

runs the risk of underestimating the severity of the depression. Implicit in the act of identifying a cause is the notion of an act that can reverse the effect. This may be unrealistic, particularly for an individual who is severely depressed, and it may have the further unwanted effect of adding to their feelings of anguished guilt.

Some problems can be talked out, though it is important for sufferers themselves to be helped towards making their own decision rather than have decisions made on their behalf by an overzealous friend. It is to be hoped that a decision can be reached as to the

Depression in others – how you can help

most likely and effective source of assistance.

Know how to respond to suicidal talk. Many people are afraid of mentioning the subject in case it encourages the act. In fact most suicidal people feel relieved that they are able to discuss this. It is important, though, to be able to respond effectively to suicidal expressions. In most of us such talk will bring about a caring response and naturally this is wholly appropriate to a person contemplating suicide. Bear in mind, however, that a few individuals are prone to use manipulative threats of dire consequences, including that of suicide, in order to achieve other ends. Of course, they are more likely to behave in this way to someone very close to them, and it is very difficult to deal with. If in any doubt, it is wisest to seek help from the most appropriate professional working either within the practice or elsewhere (see also Chapter eight).

When to ask for professional help

Usually professional help will be necessary when depression and other symptoms have continued for a time beyond which 'normal' depression has previously lasted and has been accompanied by the inability of the patient to function in all the usual and necessary roles – for example, as employee, parent, spouse or friend. The purpose of help is to find out whether treatment would be expected to shorten the length of the illness and if so which of the range of specific treatments would be most suitable and likely to be most effective.

The first option should be the family doctor who, in an ideal world, would:
● be trained to recognize depression;
● have the time to provide first-line treatment him/herself (such as anti-depressant drugs; psychotherapy/counselling).

Where labour-intensive treatments, such as counselling, are required, most family doctors should be able to refer the patient quickly to other professionals, such as trained counsellors, within their practice or elsewhere who can provide them.

Chapter six
Self-help

What can we do once depression has developed in order to minimize the harmful effects on our well-being and on the people close to us? Our aims might include the following:
- limit the impact of the illness;
- shorten its duration;
- lay the foundations for a successful recovery.

While suffering from depression, we are bound to function less well in virtually everything that we attempt and it is foolish not to take this into account. We invariably find that activity of any kind demands greater physical effort, we need to concentrate harder to attend to mental tasks and we lose the enthusiasm which normally motivates us and allows us to make light of otherwise demanding activities. We have to be sparing in the way we use our limited resources.

Limit the impact of the illness

It is natural for depressed people to become less optimistic in their thinking and this of course has effects on their judgements and assessments of situations and problems. Some individuals will respond by growing excessively cautious and hesitant, but others will become impatient and make poor decisions. It is sensible to avoid having to make important judgements or final decisions, and also to avoid making plans which may be overambitious, in case this leads to failure. On the other hand, if we severely curtail our entire usual routine, we run the risk of making our problems worse through isolating ourselves from our friends and further diminishing our already faltering self-esteem by appearing to be failing at everything.

It is important to get this balance right. Friends are often in a good position to give valuable objective advice on which tasks to continue and which to leave until depression has lifted. It is important to follow as much of our usual routine as possible since it provides a purpose and a meaning to our day and is a framework upon which recovery can be built.

Try not to neglect your physical health. Although you may not have much appetite, try to make yourself eat regularly. Try smaller but nutritious and tempting meals instead of heavier ones; treat yourself to favourite foods. Many depressed people snack and eat unhealthy foods because they cannot face full meals that they would normally enjoy. Although there is no evidence linking depression with diet (except in very severe cases of vitamin deficiency and gross malnutrition which are seldom encountered in industrialized countries), irregular diet can have

Self-help

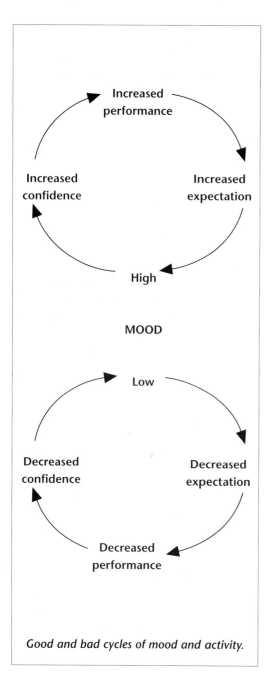

Increased
performance

Increased
expectation

High

Increased
confidence

MOOD

Low

Decreased
confidence

Decreased
expectation

Decreased
performance

Good and bad cycles of mood and activity.

a bad effect on mood and can cause further weight loss and weakness. Binge eating, as frequently occurs in eating disorders such as anorexia nervosa and bulimia, is associated with feelings of guilt and can have a similar effect if used as a source of comfort when you are depressed. Try at the same time to do some regular physical exercise, even though this may be demanding, since it maintains a routine and provides an area where activities can be completed and confidence maintained.

If you are depressed, make a special effort to take regular exercise.

People who suffer recurrently from depression report how difficult it is to convince yourself that the depression is a temporary state, that it will pass, that things will get better. Despite the logic of this argument, as well as sufferers' past experience of improvement and the known fact that depression does not last forever, it is often of little help when you are actually in its grip. Nevertheless try to keep telling yourself that things will in the future be better and take every opportunity to discuss your worries with others.

This notion has led directly to the development of a type of therapy for depression known as cognitive therapy. The principle of this treatment is simple and involves the challenging of patients' automatic beliefs concerning their ability and value, which are generally unreasonably low in individuals suffering from an episode of depression. The replacement of these automatic and pessimistic views with ones which are consistent with the evidence as seen by other people can be expected to lead to an improvement in confidence and mood. When depression is present at a later time, it may be possible to use again the principles of these techniques without the assistance of a professional or at the earliest signs of a relapse into depression, and in this way successfully begin your own therapy.

When depressed it is all too easy to feel overwhelmed by the smallest setback and to overestimate the size of problems. If we consider individual problems in isolation, they tend to appear less threatening. One useful

Helping yourself through depression

- Scale back your activities (such as work commitments) and avoid important decisions if you can.
- Deal with stress effectively.
- Tell yourself that depression does not last forever.
- Take the opportunity to discuss your worries with family and friends – they may not be solved, but you may feel better.
- Try to do as much as you feel able without undue effort – including seeing family and friends, even if for only short periods.
- Look after your hygiene and physical health and diet.
- Limit alcohol consumption.

course of action has been called a problem-solving approach and again the principles of this technique may help anyone who is depressed. Problems where solutions are reasonably within reach can be prioritized before problems which are further out of reach. You could, for example, establish a regular routine of rising, washing and performing household tasks before progressing to the more demanding activities such as preparing food or attending work or leisure pursuits.

Depressed people tend to avoid contact with their friends. They feel uncomfortable,

Self-help

It is important to maintain contact with friends when you are depressed.

unable to participate fully and are painfully aware that they are a drag on others' enjoyment. When depressed try not to avoid all contact with others, which may lead to a vicious circle of increased anxiety at exposure to these situations. Instead allow yourself shorter periods of contact and stick to people you know well and are relaxed with.

Many sufferers from depression, particularly when it is long-standing or recurrent, find that joining a formal support group is helpful. Not only is this a source of information, but being among others whom you know have shared similar experiences is a very supportive experience. Talking to others about how they have coped with depression allows you to learn from their experience directly and to take some of these strategies and perhaps adapt their use to your particular situation.

The principles of such groups is embodied in a more formal sense in the case of the psychotherapy group, where a group of people agree to meet on a regular basis over a fixed period of time in order to address problems that they hold in common. A list of organizations which facilitate the development of such support groups can be found on page 78.

Shorten the duration of the illness

Stress is a word that is frequently used in relation to depression and is often seen as a cause of it. We are all exposed to stress in our lives in many different forms. Stress takes the form of demands upon our time, our energies, our patience, our understanding and our physical resources. The other side of the stress 'coin' is interest, stimulation, achievement, interaction (with other people) and excitement, without which our lives would be impoverished. Usually stress becomes distress, which may then develop into depression if a situation arises where you are asked to do too much and take too much on. There are ways of dealing with stress that reduce its potentially harmful capacity. Learning how and when to say no, being able to delegate to others, and managing your time effectively will all reduce the likelihood of stress developing into a problem.

Many sufferers from depression find that joining a support group is helpful.

There are some clear precautions that we can take, however, while depressed. Try not to respond to depression by drinking. The use of alcohol to reverse feelings of boredom or tension can create a vicious circle of disruption of sleep and further depression of mood which will make matters worse. Unfortunately this is an easy thing to do: alcohol is freely available and in the short term may help us feel brighter and more confident. Yet its consumption leads to a longer-term further depression of mood, quite apart from its other physically damaging long-term effects. The link between alcohol misuse and depression is strong. In the short term alcohol acts as a stimulant and produces feelings of well-being – this is why it is used at social gatherings; in the period beyond a couple of hours, though, it becomes a depressant of the central nervous system, bringing about slowness, fatigue and lethargy, and sleepiness.

Alcohol can also and easily be the resort of the insomniac, because in larger doses it has a sedative effect. Unfortunately early sedative effects are compensated for later on in the night's sleep by periods of wakefulness and the need to pass water (alcohol consumption encourages the kidneys to excrete water and it disrupts the usual patterns of sleep).

For a group of individuals who, as part of their character, are chronically bored, dissatisfied and/or troubled, alcohol represents a faulty solution to these problems because it is only effective in the short term.In addition to this it has seriously toxic effects on the human body. Alcohol plays a large part in self-

Self-help

If you are depressed, do not resort to alcohol: it has an immediate sedative effect, but later on will cause your night's sleep to be broken and disturbed.

destructive behaviour, not only because it is associated with prolonged depressive conditions but also because it removes many of our natural inhibitions and increases the likelihood of impulsive behaviour which may lead to self-injury.

Lay the foundations for recovery

Sufferers from depression that tends to be recurrent can also consider preventive measures over a longer time scale. Patterns of behaviour that can be construed as self-defeating in the sense that they habitually fail to achieve a satisfactory result and which consequently engender depression can be altered and different coping strategies put in their place which are likely to lead to better outcomes. If, for example, an individual tends to become involved in relationships in which great demands are made upon the partner, this may lead to the premature break up of such relationships. This, of course, exposes the individual to a repeated series of negative life events which make them more likely to suffer from depression. Although some life events are unavoidable, others are clearly of our own making. People with maladaptive patterns of behaviour (those with disorders of personality style) are known to be more prone to such life events, and can often be seen almost to generate them, and are consequently more vulnerable to depression.

Chapter seven

Specialist help

Seeing the family doctor

Whenever a member of the family is ill, we tend to consult our family doctor, or general practitioner. The case of depression is no exception to this general rule. The vast majority of depressed people receiving treatment are doing so directly through their family doctor and indeed this approach has several clear advantages. First we are likely to

know our family doctor and they us, so they will be able easily to recognize the change in us and appreciate its significance. Second they are likely to be familiar with our family and our way of life. This will allow them to be aware of the circumstances and events which may be causing the depression as well as the personal and family resources which are going to be available to us during our period of convalescence and recovery.

Many people, however, mistakenly consider family doctors to be trained only in physical medicine. Increasingly family doctors have considerable experience of treating psychological problems. This begins with their period of experience of psychiatry as medical students, but in addition many have spent periods after their qualification as doctors working with psychiatrists as part of their post-graduate training in general practice. They are therefore well able to recognize depression and are trained to listen sympathetically to sufferers, but critically and with the objectivity that, with the best will in the world, family members may lack.

This may lead to a range of immediate responses. Family doctors are able to give simple directive advice on practical matters

A modern psychiatric unit.

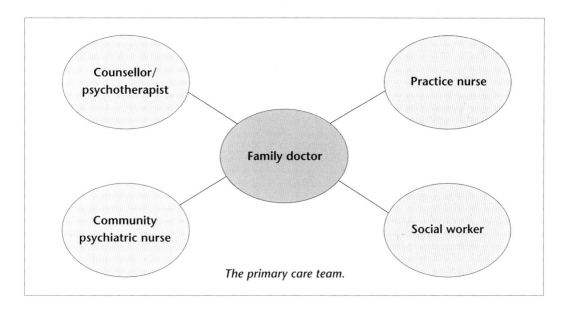

The primary care team.

which are causing concern or supportive therapy until life difficulties pass spontaneously. Family doctors have at their disposal effective simple treatments for the more severe forms of depression, for example anti-depressant drugs, but they are also well placed at the centre of a network of caring professions to arrange help from others including counsellors, psychotherapists, psychologists and social workers (known as the primary care team) and to select which of these individuals is likely to be most helpful. This is particularly relevant when considering types of treatment which are time-consuming, particularly treatments involving psychological techniques. Because of the way family doctors work and the numbers of patients that they are required to attend they are not often able to supply this sort of treatment except over relatively short periods. Increasingly, though, family doctors may employ a practice nurse or psychotherapist who has been trained in this type of work and with whom the practice works very closely.

Seeing a specialist

The family doctor, as well as providing a first port of call for all problems, is also able to filter out cases which for one or a variety of reasons justify the involvement of a specialist. These might have failed to respond to simple or first-line methods, they may be complicated by other problems, medical or otherwise, or they may require a specific type of intervention not

Specialist help

A consultation with a mental health professional.

readily available in general medical practice. In addition all family doctors have the option of referring patients to local specialist mental health services. The reasons for this might include advice on either the assessment of your problems or the best form of treatment that could subsequently be arranged by your family doctor. Alternatively it may be so that you can receive a more specialized form of treatment not available within general practice which allows greater care and support than can be arranged at home with your family.

Such specialist services generally involve doctors specializing in the diagnosis and treatment of mental illnesses (psychiatrists) as well as other disciplines including clinical psychologists, social workers and community psychiatric nurses, all of whom have particular areas of expertise in the treatment of mental health problems. Such a multi-disciplinary arrangement has developed from the notion that the causes of an illness such as depression (and indeed many other psychiatric disorders) are multiple. It therefore seems logical to develop a range of potentially helpful treatments and for this purpose all the disciplines with a legitimate claim to expertise may be required and are felt to have advantages. It is usual for these professionals to work as a team, so that all the expertise is available readily for any particular patient. These teams have grown up as an integral part of the hospital organization. Nowadays, however, they spend a large proportion of their time treating patients outside hospital in-patient settings, and will therefore work in family doctors' surgeries in conjunction with general practitioners and often also in patients' homes. This is consistent with the development of effective care for patients in the community, which has received a considerable boost in recent years from official government policy in the United Kingdom (and elsewhere in the developed world). It has led to services becoming more accessible and user-friendly and recognizes the notion of treating most patients for most of the time outside a hospital setting so that their daily life is disrupted as little as possible by their illness.

What will happen?

Whomever you see will naturally have received some information about you from your family doctor. This might be in written form or, increasingly, where a close working relationship

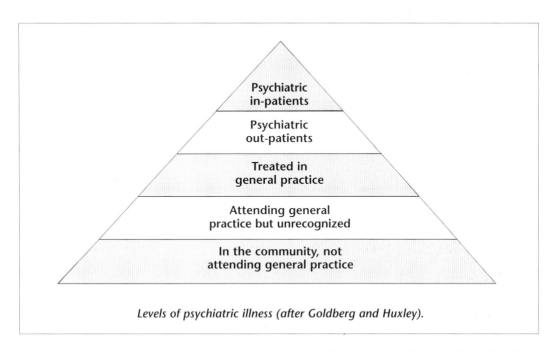

Levels of psychiatric illness (after Goldberg and Huxley).

has developed, family doctors may speak directly to their specialist colleagues. They will thus have been able to state the problem precisely and what they wish for you. The specialist will want to ask you more questions, not only about your symptoms but also regarding your family, current circumstances, any medical problems in the past or currently, your ways of tackling problems and the strengths and weaknesses of your personality. This will allow an accurate diagnosis of your condition and an appreciation of the potential causes of your illness. In turn this will lead naturally to a range of treatments being proposed. More than one type of treatment and contact with more than one member of the team may be recommended. For example, a brief course of counselling or psychotherapy

A multi-disciplinary case discussion.

53

Specialist help

(see page 70) concerning persistent or recurring relationship difficulties and how better to approach these could be given by a community nurse at the same time as a quicker-acting course of anti-depressants (see page 65) could be prescribed and monitored by your family doctor, to alleviate the most debilitating symptoms in the short term.

Psychiatrists use many of the same techniques for treating their patients as are available to family doctors. Normally as specialists they have greater experience of patients with illnesses such as depression. Depression is in fact one of the most frequent conditions treated by psychiatrists who would expect to see several dozen cases every year in the course of their normal practice. A family doctor by contrast would see very much less depression than this. Specialists are therefore more familiar with its treatment, including some forms of treatment which require particularly intensive periods of training. These are generally unavailable to family doctors because of the length of time taken in training. Psychiatrists may also be required to evaluate a case of depression which is difficult to diagnose.

Psychiatrists and their colleagues in the specialist mental health services also have access to facilities where more intensive treatment and support can be provided. Many services nowadays have a day hospital, open during office hours, where patients are invited to come for a whole day or part of a day, and can do so on a regular basis over a period of a few weeks while receiving help and recovering from their depression. This setting usually provides a range of group activities, some of a very practical nature such as art groups or woodworking classes. Others are more inclined to discussions of emotive issues, or are geared to improving coping skills such as how to manage anxiety, improving social skills or assertiveness training.

Also available are in-patient places in hospital. These are usually reserved for the relatively small group of depressed patients who have very severe symptoms, when there is real and persistent concern about their ability to care for themselves, in terms of eating and drinking sufficiently, maintaining hygiene, and the threat of active suicide attempts.

There is a potentially wide range of treatments available which will help symptoms of depression over a time course of a few weeks.

The multi-disciplinary mental health team.

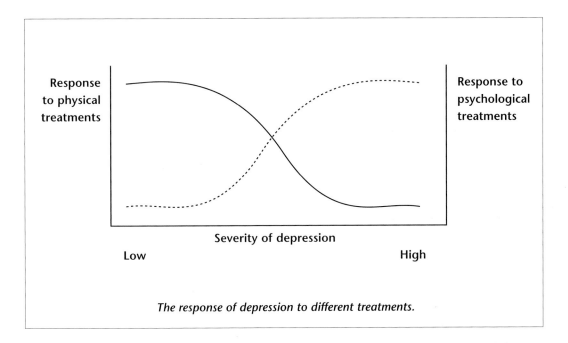

Response to physical treatments

Response to psychological treatments

Severity of depression

Low

High

The response of depression to different treatments.

Which one is selected depends not only on the characteristics of the depression and what may be causing it, but also on the type of person the patient is. For many cases of depression either talking treatments or drug treatments may be expected to be equally useful. Often in this case the preference of the patient is the deciding factor. Frequently, of course, it is both desirable and necessary for more than one approach to be pursued at the same time, and this seems to have a beneficial cumulative effect rather than the treatments opposing each other.

Generally the more serious the depression, the more likely it is to be treated with drugs. Not only are some depressed people so low and lacking in energy that they cannot command the effort to engage sufficiently in a talking form of treatment, but drug treatments often have a more rapid effect. Drug treatments are particularly effective where somatic symptoms are troublesome. They also demand that the patient is able to reflect upon himself or herself in an objective and dispassionate way: something that with the best will in the world all of us cannot always manage. There is also the group of patients who may derive benefit from electro-convulsive therapy (ECT), which is valued by psychiatrists as a rapidly acting, safe and effective method of treating severe cases of depression, particularly when it threatens life.

Psychological treatments generally involve a collaborative partnership between patient and therapist and therefore make relatively greater demands upon the time and commitment of the patient.

Specialist help

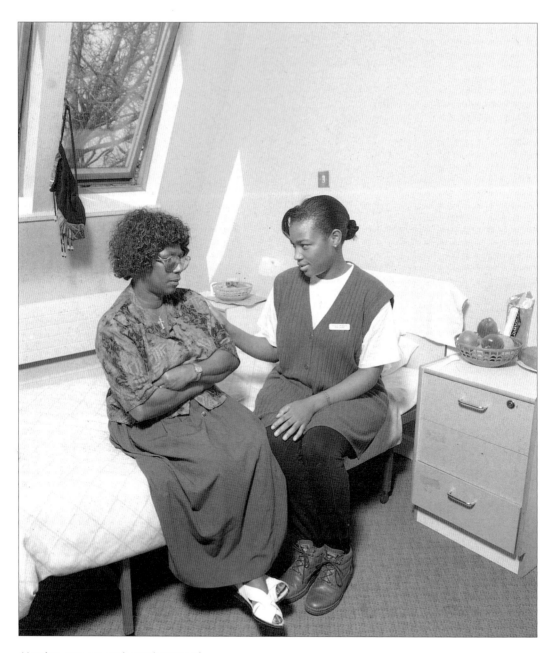

Nursing care on an in-patient ward.

Electro-convulsive therapy (ECT)

ECT is a treatment currently in use for severe depression. It involves the deliberate provocation of an epileptic fit by the passage of a small electric current between two electrodes placed on the scalp of the patient. It is, of course, attracting a degree of controversy with calls for its use to be restricted or abolished.

ECT was first widely used in the 1940s. At this time very few alternative treatments for the more severe forms of mental illness, such as mania, depression and schizophrenia, were available (drug treatments which revolutionized the management of these conditions were still some years n the future). Partly as a result of this, ECT was used for the treatment of conditions for which more acceptable alternatives are now available. Research since this time has also allowed psychiatrists to define more clearly patients who will benefit from ECT and those who will not, and this has contributed to its more restricted and targeted use nowadays. The techniques associated with its administration have also changed, with all patients being fully anaesthetized and the routine use of muscle relaxants to reduce the physical manifestations of the fit.

ECT is now used for the treatment of severe depressive illness, particularly when directly life-threatening where the fact that it acts more quickly than drug treatments is most valuable. It can also be used in the treatment of certain types of schizophrenia and in mania, though this is less common in practice. As such it is a very valuable form of treatment for a small group of patients with severe and potentially life-threatening illnesses. Although the exact mechanism of action is not known, it is a very safe treatment which has no serious or irreversible side effects. Long-term effects on memory are often claimed, but recent research into those patients receiving ECT has not supported this view.

Chapter eight

Depression and suicide

Suicide is a difficult area to deal with. Death by suicide is obviously a tragedy in the same way as any untimely death. In addition a suicide is likely to provoke strong feelings (of responsibility) in those around the person who has died. Everyone searches back through their recent contacts with the person and asks themselves what they could have done differently that might have averted the tragedy. Some feel guilty abut minor criticisms they made which they feel might have been taken to heart and been the last straw for the individual.

Society's view of suicide reflects this uncertainty. Not so long ago suicide was illegal. Although this sounds ludicrous, it may at the time have been felt to be a deterrent to some. The notion that suicide was anti-social was even more explicit in earlier times when it was felt to be a manifestation of the work of the devil perverting the thoughts and actions of sinners: suicides were deprived of the sacraments and their property subject to confiscation by the state. Despite our more liberal views today, suicide still bears a moral stigma.

Suicidal behaviour is associated with several psychiatric conditions, although depression is probably the most common. The association with depression is important not only for this reason, but also because a great deal can be done for individuals suffering from the illness. Their depressed condition remains a very temporary state. This is, however, not necessarily true for more chronic and long-lasting conditions such as alcoholism and personality disorder which are also associated with suicide.

Can we predict suicide?

Prediction of suicidal behaviour is uncertain and inexact, particularly over lengthy periods of time. Certain characteristics of an individual are associated with successful suicide. They include factors which are not readily subject to change and therefore may be of limited use in the prevention of an individual suicide.

Examples include male rather than female sex; age (generally the trend increases with age); social class; and occurrence of previous suicidal behaviour. On the other hand there are several more immediate predictors of suicide which are useful to doctors in prevention. Over the short term these have more to do with the

---

Statistical risk factors for suicide

- Male sex.
- Older age.
- Single status, particularly if recent – that is, through divorce or bereavement.

- Current physical ill health, particularly if painful, debilitating or life-threatening.
- Previous acts of deliberate self-harm.
- History of depressive illness.
- Alcohol use to excess.

---

motivation underlying an act of self-destruction and the seriousness of the intent. They are connected with the state of mind of the individual, and are therefore more subject to change over a given period of time. They are also the factors that anyone called upon to assess the risk of suicide in the immediate future must rely upon.

How common are suicidal thoughts?

Suicidal thoughts are common among the general population. Thoughts of self-destruction are entertained by the majority of people at particular moments in their lives. This is generally at times of intense disappointment or frustration when we can become overwhelmed by feelings of hopelessness. For most of us these thoughts are fleeting and pass before we can even begin to act upon them. However, if such thoughts are persistent, as may well be the case in someone who suffers from depression, plans may be formulated and put into action. Occasionally such plans may become quite elaborate and involve precautions against detection or interference in order to increase their chance of success. This situation is dangerous and requires intervention from others to protect the individual.

There is also a group of individuals who repeatedly seek to harm themselves in a way which suggests that their intent at the time was relatively high, although the people around them are astonished at how quickly this intent passes and is replaced by a casual and light-hearted attitude. Of course, in other instances the outcome is not so happy, because the behaviour of these individuals is in reality very dangerous and they sometimes succeed.

The actual seriousness of the suicide attempt supplies some information about the intent of the individual but it is important to differentiate the actual risk from the risk that was apparent to the individual. An overdose of tablets which are in fact quite safe may have been regarded by the person who took them as dangerous, and their next overdose might not turn out to be quite so innocuous.

Feelings of extreme anguish and the

Depression and suicide

Most people entertain thoughts of self-destruction at some point in their life, but generally these pass before we can even begin to act upon them.

experience of what sound to be actively unpleasant states of mood that are a source of constant pain may push a person to attempt suicide if only as a means of seeking peace. Suicidal people sometimes talk about this as going to sleep. Beliefs of complete futility, hopelessness and utter unrelieved gloom are dangerous, as are strong feelings of personal responsibility, blame, sinfulness, wickedness and of being deserving of punishment. In the small proportion of severely depressed people where contact with reality is lost, sufferers may experience insulting or derogatory hallucinated voices which repeat the sinfulness of the individual and may urge or command suicide. All these factors are indicative of a real risk of suicide and it is imperative that the person be protected from themselves.

Immediate risk factors for suicide

Someone is regarded as an immediate suicide risk if he or she is currently:
- experiencing severely depressed mood;
- hallucinating commands to commit suicide;
- hopeless and pessimistic;
- self-blaming and guilty;
- expressing intent to harm himself or herself.

A person is also regarded as an immediate suicide risk after a suicidal act if this entailed:
- careful preparation of the act;
- precautions to avoid interruption or rescue;
- a suicide note and an 'ordering' of personal affairs;
- the expectation of the method being fatal;
- remorse at the failure of the act.

How to respond to expressions of suicidal intent

What should you do if someone tells you that they are contemplating suicide, or you have asked them and they have responded in this way? First of all try not to be alarmed or embarrassed. Accept this information calmly and encourage the individual to explain further why and how they intend to commit suicide. There is a notion that suicidal talk is a cry for help, and although this is undoubtedly true in the sense that suicidal behaviour is generally the last resort of someone in an intolerable situation, it cannot be relied upon not to be meant quite seriously and literally.

Some factors tend to prevent people from putting suicidal thoughts into practice and are therefore relatively reassuring if referred to. Worries about distressing loved ones, or leaving dependent children vulnerable are protective. So are thoughts of the sinfulness of suicide and notions of shame. Fear of physical disability or mutilation as a result of an unsuccessful and violent attempt can deter up to a point.

In the majority of cases suicidal thoughts are temporary, although the tragedy of course is that during this temporary period permanent injury or indeed death may be brought about. Much effort is currently being devoted to programmes of suicide prevention by health authorities and other organizations. This involves a wide range of activities, among them: encouraging those in depression to seek help, and making it more accessible, including informal sources of help such as the Samaritans; and incorporating safety features into railways, bridges and buildings. If the impulse to suicide can be frustrated, even for a a matter of minutes, there is a greater chance that suicide will be avoided.

Chapter nine

Understanding depression and its treatment

Understanding what causes depression is important for more than one reason. Knowledge of the mechanisms through which an individual becomes depressed help in the search for effective treatments. It may in time lead to advances in prevention of depression, including identifying those most at risk of the illness.

The field of mental health receives contributions from many areas of science and thought, including medicine, other biological sciences, experimental psychology, sociology, theoretical psychology and others. Each of these approaches has its own validity and none has all the answers or is the "right' way. Rather all attempt to examine the same phenomenon but from different theoretical standpoints. The result is that all mental illnesses can be envisaged as the final result of many interacting factors present in proportions varying depending upon the individual circumstances of the case. This is particularly true of an illness such as depression where the severity and character of the depression can be so variable, and the range of factors that are important in its creation are so many.

Genetic factors

It has long been known that in the families of sufferers from depression, particularly the more severe and recurrent forms, there occur more cases than would be expected according to the general population rates of these illnesses. The likelihood of a family member of a depression sufferer also suffering at some point in their life is influenced by the closeness of their blood relationship; in other words the proportion of genetic material shared by the two individuals. Although, of course, individuals sharing the same family also share much of their physical and social environment, particularly in the early years of development, careful study has shown that vulnerability to depression can be passed on by specific genes. It would be simplistic to suggest that there is a gene or even a group of genes which programme an individual to suffer

Research has shown that vulnerability to depression can be hereditary.

from depression: clearly, not least because studies reveal that even closely related individuals may still have differing predilections for suffering from depression, other factors intervene or modify this causal progression. The most acceptable current model of genetic influence on depression is that several genes are implicated in conferring characteristics (personality traits, such as anxiousness or impulsiveness, or constitutional attributes, such as proneness to physical ill health) which cause a degree of vulnerability. When these are exposed to other interactive factors (physical, psychological or social), the combination may trigger an episode of depression.

Knowledge of an individual's family and genetic background is helpful in reaching accurate diagnosis in difficult cases and in advising prospective parents who suffer from severe forms of depression on the risk of illness in their children. There is no treatment available which can eradicate genetic traits. However, in future the possibilities of manipulation of genetic material to replace it with material that will not pass on the clear vulnerability for recurrent depression will undoubtedly increase. This at present is not technically possible.

Understanding depression and its treatment

Physical factors

Symptoms indistinguishable from depression have been described in a variety of medical conditions for which there is a very clearly understood causative physical mechanism. These include localized illnesses affecting the central nervous system (for instance, Parkinson's disease) to more general so-called systemic illnesses affecting all parts of the body (for example, viral infections such as glandular fever). A list of those most commonly involved is given in the box below.

Because depression may occur in the context of another illness or illnesses, it is usual to expect that if treatment of this illness successfully alleviates it, the depression will improve at the same time. These observations have direct relevance for treatment in only a small number of cases, however. Such observations have also sparked a whole series of speculative theories about the causes of depression or, in a more restricted sense, the mediation of the bodily and mental effects of depression by particular physiological systems known to operate in the human body. The most obvious examples of this would be the hormonal or endocrine system and the network of nerve pathways known to make up the central nervous system and the transmission of electrical signals along them.

This general approach, as well as more specific observations, has led to remarkable developments in the treatments available for depression, a fact that is easily overlooked currently, particularly in the light of the present lay fashion to regard all depression, as well as other psychological disturbances, as having a psychologically understandable cause.

In the 1950s it became possible to begin to

Physical disorders causing depression

Infections
- Glandular fever
- HIV infection

Endocrine and metabolic disorders
- Myxoedema (thyroid deficiency)
- Cushing's disease (adrenal gland overactivity)
- Parathyroid overactivity

Cerebral disorders
- Stroke

- Parkinson's disease
- Multiple sclerosis

Generalized disorders
- Anaemia
- Widespread/metastatic cancer

Drugs
- Cortisone
- Anti-hypertensive drugs, such as alpha methyl-dopa
- Alcohol

investigate the group of chemicals, subsequently known as neuro-transmitters, which regulated the electrical activity of the brain. Their role in conducting electrical impulses between nerve cells was already amply demonstrated in the control of relatively straightforward activity such as the movement of voluntary muscles and the reception of simple sensations such as sound. The next step was to investigate their role in the creation of the thoughts, intentions, moods and so forth that represent the more complicated conscious activity of the human mind. Particular chemicals have been implicated as being important in specific areas of the brain and are assumed to be involved in the functions represented by these areas of the brain. This incidentally draws on a rather older notion, as manifest in the nineteenth-century discipline of phrenology, that different areas of the brain are responsible for discrete functions of the mind such as mood or thought.

At about the same time doctors treating patients with high blood pressure in the 1950s observed that treatment with certain drugs tended to cause depression. The common factor of these drugs seemed to be their effects on the metabolism of a particular group of chemicals known as biogenic amines and this led to close examination of the location of these chemicals in the brain of normal and depressed individuals. Later it became possible to develop a range of drugs specifically designed to interfere with the metabolism of these same chemicals and increase their presence in the brain. These drugs have proved to be effective anti-depressant agents and have been used widely and successfully in the treatment of depression since the late 1950s. A great deal is now known about the effects of these drugs and who is likely to benefit most from them.

Anti-depressant drugs are usually prescribed in courses of four to six weeks in the treatment of depression. It is an unfortunate characteristic of all these drugs that there is a delay in the onset of their therapeutic effect of at least two weeks from the beginning of treatment. Side effects, however, begin earlier, with the result that some patients feel worse before they get better and may therefore stop taking drugs. Happily the vast majority of side effects are not serious or dangerous and more often present patients with irritating or nuisance effects, which despite their depressed condition they may find tolerable. Thus one of the main tasks of a doctor prescribing anti-depressants is to support and encourage a patient to endure during this period. Some of these drugs, especially the older ones, have been shown to have potentially serious side effects, particularly affecting the rhythms of the heart. This is not generally a problem at normal therapeutic doses, but becomes potentially dangerous in overdoses, as of course is a possibility in depressed patients. It is also important with patients with pre-existing heart disease. Doctors now have a range of relatively safe drugs to use which are preferable.

Anti-depressant drugs are often confused by lay people with drugs which have anti-anxiety and sleep-inducing properties, particularly the benzodiazepines. These drugs are not used as treatments for depression as they have no effect on its main symptoms. However, part of the confusion is because the benzodiazepines may

Understanding depression and its treatment

How anti-depressant drugs are grouped

The original forms of anti-depressant drugs, developed and first used in the 1950s, have subsequently been refined in the development of new compounds, though some of the original tried and tested drugs are still in use. They act by boosting the levels of particular chemicals in the brain which act as neuro-transmitter chemicals and which, evidence suggests, are temporarily deficient in the brains of individuals suffering from depression. They are quite separate in their chemical make-up and their mode of action from drugs known as minor tranquillizers, which as the name suggests are used as primarily anti-anxiety or sleep-inducing agents and which include the benzodiazepine group of drugs such as valium.

The anti-depressant drugs can be divided into several groups depending on the exact neuro-transmitter chemical they principally affect and also on which mechanism is employed to achieve the desired effect. They tend mainly to differ in the profile of side effects that they produce, there being little evidence that any particular group has major advantages over other groups in terms of their therapeutic effect. All these drugs will help about two-thirds of depressed patients over a period of three to four (occasionally more) weeks and bring about improvement in mood, sleep, appetite and energy levels.

Anti-depressant drugs are typically considered in the following groupings:

Tricyclic anti-depressants
Available since the early 1960s, some of the earlier representatives of this class have now been superseded by other drugs of the same or a different class. Their main problem is adverse effects including cardiac dangers for those with previous heart disease or when taken in overdose. They are nevertheless tried and tested, having been in use for 30 years, and newer versions have less problematic side effects.

Mono-amine oxidase inhibitors (MAOIs)
The earliest group of drugs developed, MAOIs have interactions which are potentially severe with foodstuffs and other drugs and these therefore need to be avoided, hence the dietary restrictions necessary. They seem to be more effective for types of depression where anxiety symptoms are prominent.

Specific serotonin re-uptake inhibitors (SSRIs)
Serotonin is a brain neuro-transmitter which has received a great deal of scientific scrutiny in recent years and is felt to be heavily involved in the cause of depression. As a result drugs which specifically affect this neuro-transmitter have been developed. As such they have the advantage of fewer side effects than older drugs, but do not appear to bring about a therapeutic effect more quickly or reliably.

Miscellaneous

Included here are drugs acting on neuro-transmitter systems other than those affected by the groups of drugs listed above, or where the mechanism of action is obscure, and as such they represent a very mixed bag. They comprise drugs like lithium, which was fortuitously discovered to have a long-term mood-stabilizing effect which has been employed to the advantage of long-term sufferers from manic-depressive illnesses, and atypical conventional anti-depressants such as mianserin and tryptophan.

These drugs can be used in combination, though this is not necessary in the vast majority of illnesses. They can readily be prescribed by family doctors and are typically used in courses of six to eight weeks, after which a continuation period of several months may be recommended to avoid early relapse. Anti-depression drug use does not lead to dependence or addictions.

Examples of anti-depressant drugs

Tricyclic drugs
- Imipramine
- Amitryptiline
- Dothiepin
- Lofepramine

Mono-amine oxidase inhibitors (MAOIs)
- Phenelzine
- Tranylcypromine
- Moclobemide

'Second-generation' anti-depressants
- Mianserin
- Trazodone
- Viloxazine

Selective serotonin re-uptake inhibitors (SSRIs)
- Fluvoxamine
- Fluoxetine (prozac)
- Sertraline
- Paroxetine

Miscellaneous drugs
- Lithium
- Carbamazepine

resolve some of the symptoms found in depression, such as insomnia and anxiety, while not affecting others such as low mood or loss of appetite. The other difference is that anti-depressants are not addictive whereas benzodiazepines can quite easily become so.

Factors in early life

From around the turn of the nineteenth century well-known theoretical psychologists, such as Freud, examining depression have taken as their starting point the theme of loss which seems an indisputable part of the illness. What is meant by this can be seen if we consider the loss of value that depressed persons see in themselves and their surroundings, their loss of hope and aspiration, the loss of energy and vitality. In its most complete and pure expression individuals may, concretely and literally, deny their own existence. These patients are said to suffer from delusions of nihilism, and this is characteristic of the most severe forms of depression.

A sense of loss

Writers who have considered the early psychological world of the young child have differed in detail, but they generally include concepts of valued objects, usually the parents, which can be used as models or stereotypes upon which the development of further relationships are based. If a parent or both parents are lost, either literally through separation or death, or metaphorically by being regarded as absent or unsympathetic at critical junctures, the model becomes distorted. This affects not only the child's view of others in the world, but also the place and value of the child itself within its concept of the world. At times in the future, in the face of particular circumstances in relation to others or other experiences, the original loss can be revived and re-experienced and manifest itself as a disabling period of depression.

Further support for these theories can be gathered from observations of animals and children separated from their parents at particular stages of development, and much has been written on experimental and observational psychology in this area. Sociologists have also contributed the findings that significant early loss events, such as the death of parents, seem to be more associated with depression in later life than chance would predict.

These theoretical approaches have led to a range of psychotherapeutic interventions, which involve mentally re-experiencing, within a trusting and confidential relationship with the therapist, many of the experiences of early childhood with the expectation of emotional relief and intellectual insight. These treatments tend to be lengthy and are therefore often reserved for patients with more persistent depression which is, however, less disabling on a day-to-day basis. Unfortunately, they are often allocated on the basis of fad, fashion and ability to pay. Interest is developing in briefer

Freud and his followers believed that traumatic events in childhood could have profound effects on the mental health of the adult individual.

forms of treatment which might be available to larger groups of patients. And of course such principles also inform group therapies which may therefore be less scarce resources than individual therapy. Other forms of group psychotherapy include working specifically with couples and with families, where issues may be relevant in the depression of one member. In all these forms of therapy the principles and the objective, the achievement of insight and understanding, remain similar.

Psychological theories have also influenced our concepts of personality development. Personality is known to be important in causing depression in that the illness is more common in those with marked personality traits. This may be because those with a less-than-ideal personality have fewer friends to support them when they have problems, or because the self-defeating behaviour which is a

Understanding depression and its treatment

Psychotherapy

Psychotherapy is a term which can be applied to a very wide range of interventions and treatments used to help sufferers from mental health problems of all sorts, including depression. It encompasses all types of treatment where two individuals (a therapist and a patient) collaborate together to address a problem presented by the patient. This usually entails a commitment by both parties to a series of meetings, often on a regular basis, in a setting associated with the care of ill people, in order to further this aim.

The exact techniques employed vary with the training of the therapist and the requirements of the patient. Some of the commoner forms of psychotherapy include: supportive psychotherapy concentrating on exploring the nature of problems, encouragement and advice in the context of some degree of understanding of the patient's difficulties (arguably all health professionals' contacts with their patients would include such an element); directive counselling, where specific strategies can be considered to tackling problems; interpretive or psychodynamic psychotherapy, where the verbal material presented by the patient is interpreted by the therapist in order to shed light on the persistent problems the patient is encountering, awareness of which is usually outside the conscious appreciation of the patient; and cognitive behavioural psychotherapy, where the behaviour and thoughts of the patient are analysed with a view to altering them in order to seek better ways of dealing with common situations. Some psychotherapies can be delivered in an individual one-to-one setting and others in small groups, including couples, as in marital therapy and families in family therapy.

Among other factors shared by all these types of therapy are an agreement by the patient to commit himself or herself to the process and the contract, and the expectation that results are not likely to appear immediately. They therefore require hard work and a degree of patience from the patient before gains are acheived, and from the professional's point of view careful selection of who is likely to benefit.

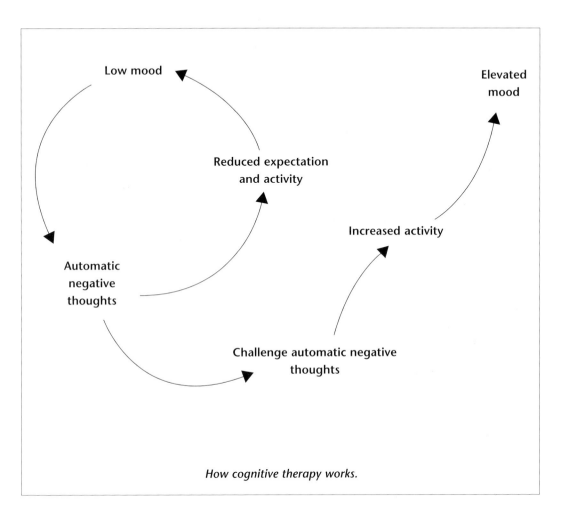

How cognitive therapy works.

characteristic of this group seems to generate adverse life events. One fruitful line of thought began with the so-called learned helplessness theory of Seligman. This was originally derived from experimental psychology, where experimental animals who had no control over events, such as whether they received a reward, or more pointedly whether they received a painful stimulus such as an electrical shock, became apathetic and inactive, a state resembling depression in humans. Likewise human beings placed in a distressing situation, the resolution of which was beyond their control, may lapse into a state of withdrawn detachment and lack of involvement akin to depression. Repeated exposure to such unsatisfactory situations during the critical periods of personality development, assumed to be in childhood, might lead to unsuccessful and self-defeating patterns of coping in stressful situations, such that their distress and depression was perpetuated and magnified.

This has led to useful treatments, the most developed of which is known as cognitive therapy. This technique involves examining the automatic assumptions that individuals make about their abilities on the basis of quite restricted information, but upon which they nevertheless base their judgements and actions. Challenging these assumptions opens the way for alternative views of ability, better performance and consequent improvement in mood and other related symptoms. This is shown in the diagram on page 71.

Life events and vulnerability factors

Researchers investigating depression have often noted the association between unusual events in life and the subsequent onset of depression. This of course is not an unexpected association given our experience of life. It has become clear that certain types of these so-called life events, especially those which involve a loss (of a friend, a valued belief or hope, for example) or an increase in expectation or responsibilities, are particularly potent. The former would include bereavement, physical ill health, losing a job and a relationship ending. The latter might include promotion, having a baby, moving house or changing jobs. It is also true that these are all common experiences and not everyone encountering them falls ill with depression.

This has led to the idea that, for various reasons, some people may be more vulnerable than others to such adverse life events. These reasons could include the heredity, make-up and physical constitution of the individual, personality, the individual's network of social support and other social factors such as accommodation and finances. Problems in these areas can make a person more susceptible, and conversely positive factors may represent a protective element. For example, having a small network of supportive friends in whom we can confide is often regarded as a protective factor against depression.

In terms of practical treatment, although it is not possible to predict specific life events in advance, it is clear that an individual's habitual approach to problems or opportunities, if persistently failing in its purpose, may actually generate adverse life events. It is, therefore, in theory possible to alter the way we do things so that this outcome becomes less likely.

Many of the vulnerability factors that have been proposed have more to do with the individual's social environment, and treatment may therefore pursue current difficulties in the realm of relationships, housing, work and finance with consequent beneficial effects for the person concerned. Such treatments might include training in social skills, anxiety management and assertiveness, and bear many resemblances to the forms of intervention that we recognize as formal psychotherapies.

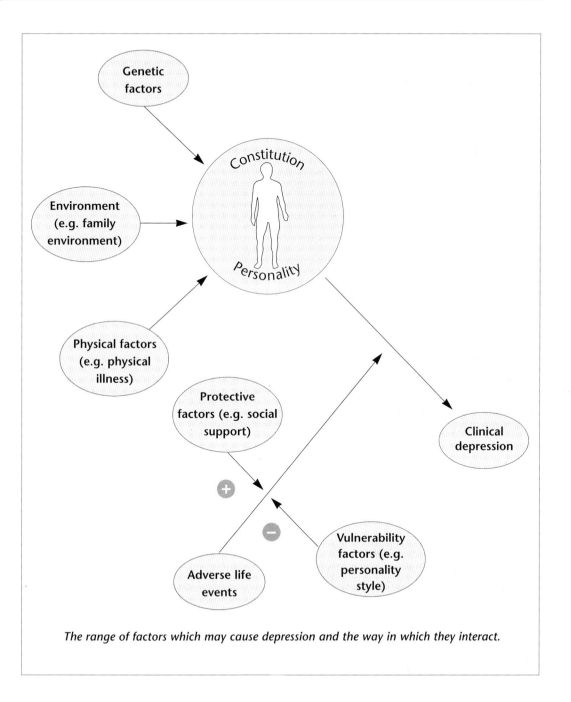

The range of factors which may cause depression and the way in which they interact.

Chapter ten
Recovery and getting back to normal

Depression that is severe enough to warrant treatment is very likely to improve completely. Often, however, this can take some time: although someone treated for depression will usually start to feel better after as little as two to three weeks, their recovery will continue over a slightly longer period, perhaps lasting several months, before all their symptoms are improved. During this time of convalescence there are some pointers to achieving an optimal recovery.

Once he or she is beginning to feel better, it is important that the person considers carefully the amount and type of activity that he or she is able to do. The ideal would be to increase the amount and complexity of tasks gradually, week by week, being careful to keep the progression but without setting overambitious targets. With the achievement of smaller steps, confidence will gradually be restored: the risk of larger steps which an individual may fail to achieve is that this will damage the recovering confidence.

Structuring the day into small achievable tasks adjusts this principle to a day-by-day level and will prevent the potentially damaging experience of failure, while at the same time introducing a reassuring certainty into the routine. Family and friends can often help by sharing the burden as new activities are returned to the sufferer. At work an early return to routine can be facilitated by colleagues temporarily taking on a greater-than-usual share of the workload.

What should you tell your friends?

Owning up to depression potentially places you in a vulnerable position. Friends may misunderstand, think that you are weak or lacking in determination, or on the other hand seriously mentally ill or in the longer run unreliable. It is wise to tell only people you really trust. Telling someone is important (as discussed in Chapter six) and having confidants is a protection against depression as well as an aid to recovery. Friends being aware of how depression is affecting you will enable them to make allowances for your temporary inability to perform as normal, and therefore for them to compensate. Moral support and understanding of the problem cannot be overestimated.

74

When you return to work, colleagues can help initially by sharing some of your workload.

Telling your employer

People often worry about informing their employer because of the concern about their longer-term job prospects. In the ideal world employers should treat depression no differently from other health problems which require time off work such as minor injuries, chest infections, menstrual difficulties and all the other common medical complaints. Employers can be of great value in allowing an employee to return to work gradually, adjusting their workload or allowing part-time work, for example. Unfortunately it is true that many employers are worried that depression will permanently effect their employee's performance, an assumption which for the majority of sufferers from depression is simply not true. It seems important in the long run that employers are made more aware of what

Recovery and getting back to normal

depression means. While depressed people function less well, after recovery their performance in all areas, including the ability to monitor and supervise work, take judgements and decisions and to shoulder responsibility, is unaffected and their having experienced depression should not be held against them in the issues of career development or promotion to positions of responsibility.

Your doctor or your employer's occupational health service may well be able to act as a useful mediator between yourself and your employer so that a period of sickness absence, if necessary, can be followed by gradual and orderly return to work.

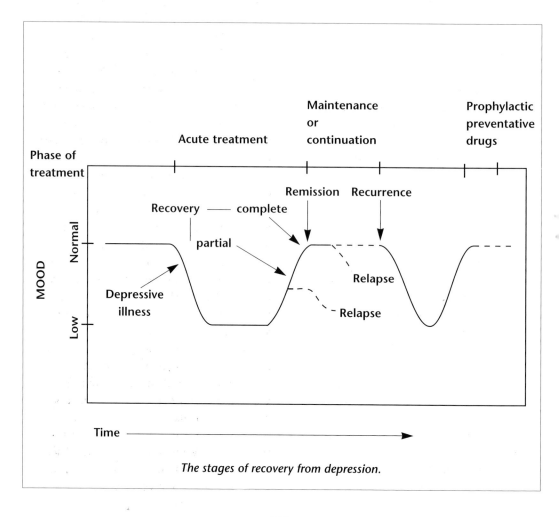

The stages of recovery from depression.

Continuing treatment

Because recovery from an episode of depression often takes place over a period of several months and because depression can be a recurrent illness, your doctor or other medical adviser may recommend continuing treatment beyond the point where you feel symptomatically recovered. It has been shown that up to half of patients who have recovered from an episode of depression may relapse again within the following six months into a state of depression, but also that continuing with anti-depressant drug treatment during this period substantially reduces this risk. There is evidence too that other treatments not involving drugs, such as some of the psychotherapies, may have a similar protective effect. Your doctor is well placed to advise on the length of treatment required, taking into account all the other relevant factors, including your life situation and your access to other forms of support.

Sometimes when an individual has suffered repeated episodes of depression – say, every year or two over a period of several years – it may be wise to consider protective or prophylactic treatment. Medical studies have shown that, in such patients prone to repeated episodes of depression, continuing with anti-depressant drugs reduces both the frequency and the severity of such recurrences. This has been particularly well demonstrated in the case of lithium carbonate and related drugs in the treatment of manic-depressive psychosis, but increasingly it seems to be equally important in recurrent forms of depression which do not involve episodes of mania.

Consideration has also recently been given to whether other forms of treatment than drugs have any ability to prevent further episodes of illness in people who might be expected to be vulnerable in this sense. The results of early studies demonstrate that certain forms of psychotherapy may also have such a beneficial effect and therefore can be considered as a valuable protective intervention. In all these instances the decision as to whether to continue treatment (of whichever form) needs to be taken by balancing the pros and cons of each course of action. Thus it is important to attempt to predict the likelihood of a further episode (predictive factors are the previous history of depression, the presence of adverse social circumstances and the likelihood of threatening life events in the future) and the severity of past episodes and the degree of disruption with which they are associated. This can then be compared with the possibility of adverse effects of treatment and the time and attention given by the patient to whichever form of treatment is most suitable. On the basis of this cost-benefit analysis a decision can be made.

Whatever the need for protective treatment and strategies, it is important for patients not to feel inhibited in their future activities. The vast majority of people who suffer an episode of depression make a complete recovery and should be able to get back to normal. They should never feel that they have to cut back on activities or aspirations – in the majority of cases this is just not necessary.

Useful addresses

Association for Post-Natal Illness
25 Jerdan Place
London SW6 1BE
Tel: 0171 386 0868
A national telephone
support scheme for those
with post-natal depression.

Defeat Depression Campaign
Royal College of Psychiatrists
17 Belgrave Square
London SW1X 1PG
Tel: 0171 235 2351

Depressives Anonymous
36 Chestnut Avenue
Beverley
Humberside HU17 9QU
Tel: 01482 860619
Organization run as a source
of support for sufferers,
complementary to
professional care.

Depression Alliance
PO Box 1022
London SE1 7QB
Information, support and
understanding for people who
suffer with depression and for
relatives who want to help.

**London Marriage
Guidance Council**
76a New Cavendish Street
London W1
Tel: 0171 580 1087

**The Manic-Depression
Fellowship**
8-10 High Street
Kingston-upon-Thames
Surrey KT1 1EY
Tel: 0181 974 6550
Network of local self-help groups
for sufferers and their families.

MIND
Granta House
15–19 Broadway
Stratford
London E15 4BQ
Tel: 0181 519 2122
Publishes a wide range
of literature on all aspects
of mental health.

**Relate (National
Marriage Council)**
Herbert Gray College
Little Church Street
Rugby
Warwickshire
CV21 3AP
Tel: 01788 573241

The Samaritans
10 The Grove
Slough
Berks SL1 1QP
Tel: 01753 532713
Voluntary organization operating
a help-line for anyone in need of
a listening ear and sympathetic
advice. Will also direct to local
caring organization if necessary.

**Seasonal Affective Disorders
Association**
PO Box 989
London SW7 2PZ
Tel: 0181 969 7028
Aims to inform and educate
people about seasonal affective
disorder (SAD). Offers advice
and support to members.

Manic Depression Fellowship
North-West
Workbase
23 New Mount Street
Manchester
M4 4DE
Tel: 0161 953 4105

Manic Depression Fellowship
Scotland
19 Elmbank Street
Glasgow
G2 4PB
Tel: 0141 248 3234

Manic Depression Fellowship
Wales
Belmont
St Cadoc's Hospital
Caerleon
Newport
Gwent
NP6 1XQ
Tel: 01633 430430

Northern Ireland Association for
Mental Health
84 University Street
Belfast
Tel: 01232 228474

AUSTRALIA

Mental Health Foundation of
Australia
Mental Health Education and
Resource Centre
Tweedie Place
Richmond
Victoria 3121

CANADA

Canadian Mental Health
Association
2160 Yonge Street
3rd Floor
Toronto
Ontario M4S 2Z3
New Zealand

Mental Health Foundation of
New Zealand
PO Box 37-438
Parnell
Aukland 1

REPUBLIC OF
SOUTH AFRICA

South African Federation for
Mental Health
210 Happiness House
PO Box 2587
Loveday &
Wolmarans Street
Johannesburg 2000

USA

National Mental Health
Association
1707 Pinto Place
Bismarck
ND

Index